CHAMELEON ON A KALEIDOSCOPE
ANONYMOUS

1

I didn't get laid enough to be called a sex addict. And yet the name felt right. In the same way a junkie spent all his time thinking about his next fix, my life had become something I did between orgasms. I joked about it, saying I was a Vagitarian but I knew it wasn't normal. Giving up booze was only the beginning. I wasn't free. The prison had just gotten bigger. But I couldn't meet girls in bars anymore. And dating within Alcoholics Anonymous was out of the question since the last thing I wanted to do was wake up beside a version of myself in a skirt. So it was ironic, that my fiancé should be the one who inadvertently introduced me to online dating.

YVETTE
Bobbing and swaying in front of my face as we ascended the steps to her fourth floor Elizabeth Street apartment was the reason we'd been together so long. Our evening stroll had been cut short by a rainstorm and so once we got inside we shook off

our wet things and lay across her bed and chatted and ordinarily this would have been enough to get the ball rolling but I was still not confident enough to make a move. Was she still pissed at me? I had work the next day and she didn't. Maybe she wanted me to leave. Time to call her bluff. While making the dramatic announcement that I had better go if I was to be in decent shape for work the next day I began to say goodbye to her magnificent world class ass.

"You hug it like it's a separate person." she said thawing a little.

"You're accusing me of having an affair with your ass, behind your back?"

A smile.

She was pissed because I hadn't picked up on her latest hint that we should live together, get married, have children and die of old age in each other's arms. These hints had more recently taken the form of exaggerated street mimes. The huge crazy-eyed smile she reserved for babies was subtle compared to the impossible affection conjured up in the presence of every old couple we encountered. Especially, for some reason, if they were Asian. I resisted the urge to respond or acknowledge because I knew that once recognised the subject could never be put back in the box. There was no way I was going to marry her but there was no way I'd be allowed access to her ass if she knew this. It was only a matter of time before something would need to be said.

I felt sufficiently encouraged by that half-hearted smile to spank her gently through her cotton knickers. This led to touching and tickling, pecking and pouting and after she broke away to brush her teeth, turn out the lights and close her laptop we progressed to sensual half-lit sensitive sex. She fluttered up and down on me with such agility I was reminded of a nymph whose gossamer wings allowed her to hover and dip at will. The rain persisted outside and as she leaned back to scratch gently under my balls the colder light from outside contrasted with the ochre glow from the desk-lamp backlighting her small perfect dancer's breasts. I stiffened inside her and her body immediately straightened as if we really had become one.

I wanted to say I love you but it was too risky. She would surely see through it for the manipulation it was and stop what she was doing. I toyed with saying you're lovely but this just felt childish. I adore you was merely I love you-lite and oh baby was completely meaningless.

"Fuck yeah." I said at last.

Well at least it was honest.

On a monthly showreel called Shotz, in the New Directors section, I was presented with the fact that a copywriter I worked with at my former agency had since become a commercials director. Nestled there amongst the self-conscious up-to-the-minute motion graphics was a link to his finished commercial, which, if it was a piece of shit would have been fine but it wasn't. It was quite good. The reason is was quite good was because it was my idea. He and I had talked about making the same commercial for BNV at Killallon Fitzpatrick but for some reason we never presented it. I think because we decided it was too British for the American market. And now adding disgust to discomfort I saw that this commercial was for Olaffson.

ack at me for
ght I was being
he guy in the
John knew I
:ause it wasn't
ial, the kind of
o show he can
nds. But this
3NV because
ey made safe
I related it to
iblic Service
A

_egan with a title.

The Beginner's Guide To Lip-Reading.

A young woman looks earnestly into the camera.

"Bastard." she says

"Bastard."she says again. Cut to an extreme close up of her mouth as she pronounces the word soundlessly now so we can recognise it when spoken.

"Bastard." she says again.

Cut now to a street-scene where a young trendy man, looking suspiciously like Jason, strolls confidently up to a new Olaffson and jabs his electronic key at the sleek crouched vehicle and disappears inside it. On the other side of the street a pale young man with a shaved head, looking suspiciously like me, watches the car drive smoothly away just as we see him say something. It's a two-syllable word. Sitting there watching the commercial I couldn't help it, the word had already left my own mouth before I realised it.

"Bastard."

A title appears across the bottom of the screen.

Everybody's Talking about the New Olaffson

I casually mentioned to Yvette that it might be a relief to get out of advertising.

"How are you going to bring up kids if you don't have a good job?"

There was no way to answer this truthfully without robbing myself of sex and so attempting to redirect the subject I told her I wanted to go back to London and write a book in my newly paid-off flat. It had been her idea to pay off the mortgage on my flat in London so that the rent received could be treated as salary and then with no rent or mortgage to pay I could always go on the dole for pocket money.

"Any man who goes on welfare by choice is a disgrace."

Obviously her vision of my future involved me working my ass off to keep her in expensive dinners and clothes. Her reaction confirmed what I was already thinking. That I should never tell her what I was thinking. My continued presence would be understood as an agreement to marry and there was no way this was ever going to happen. Up to that point I had feigned interest in whatever she pointed me at, as long as I was sexually rewarded. And the sex was so influential I had managed to convince myself I wasn't even acting. I was more than happy to pay for the restaurants, the Broadway plays and even the clothes she picked out as long as we contin-ued with our unspoken agreement that I would be sexually compensated. And for the first year we had been very fair about this distribution of sexual currency.

Her first. Then me.

But more recently a new worrying pattern had begun to emerge where my orgasm couldn't even be contemplated until she had come not just once, but twice. It was starting to feel like my second high-stress job. And it wasn't as if she was scorching hot. Yes her body was fabulous and yes she was French (that accent alone got me hard) but her face was far from perfect and I could hardly admit it to myself but she had some sort of skin problem where hard-headed yellowy protrusions would periodically emerge without warning. Why did I have to settle for that? I was living in New York where I regularly encountered four or five life-changing women on the way to the subway.

When we first met I was still reeling from the romantic catastrophe that would eventually become the subject of my first book so I wasn't even remotely looking for a girlfriend. But Yvette knew what it was to be foreign in the US and this was something that immediately drew us together. And like all Europeans we enjoyed the luxury of being able to encapsulate the world's problems in one word.

"Americans."

We rolled our eyes knowingly.

It was obvious even in her staid work clothes that there was a great body under there but I honestly didn't see her as a sexual possibility until months later. The fact that she was French was something I couldn't ignore. She loved toilet humor. Anything to do with piss or poop and she began to giggle like a sneaky schoolgirl at the back of the class. Her pet name for me was Poopie-Head. She sometimes even repeated the word during sex.

"Poopie, poopie."

She loved to show me the contents of her mouth while she ate. Especially in expensive restaurants. She'd beckon me towards her, as if she had a secret to share, with her hand supposedly directing her voice into my ear until at the last moment she'd open her mouth wide revealing mashed bouilla-baisse and bread. When I appeared sufficiently disgusted her hand morphed from horror-shield to giggle-guard and she sat back satisfied into her chair.

She was impossible to sleep with.

I'd lie motionless at three am in her moonlit bedroom her arm heavy as a fallen beam across my chest, afraid to move for fear of initiating a wee-hours discussions about how distant I was. Did I feel I was distant? Why was I always so distant?

"Distant? What? Yvette I'm right here."

Then fondling my balls she'd whisper "you're not nice with me" and I'd find myself inside her. How ridiculously easy it was to get inside a vagina when the owner actually wanted you in it. And as her weightless silhouette gyrated above me I knew better than to come. That would be the ultimate act of selfishness.

Not yet fully awake she moves like an animal sure and silent with her palms pressed flat on my chest as her groin insists itself against me scratching some unbearable, unreachable itch inside her. To prevent myself from detonating I conjure up Jason's shit-eating grin as he admires his own reflection in the monitor during the few seconds of dead space preceding each showing of his new Falfaux commercial.

My present agency wasn't capable of producing anything good enough to wipe away that grin but most New York production companies would at least listen to an idea from an on-staff creative like me working on an account like Olaffson since they were always keen to develop a relationship that might lead to a lucrative job. Above me, naked and shining Yvette might have been peering into a well.

Open on a shot of a young man who looks exactly like Jason. He's playing the part of a Olaffson dealer as he hands the keys to a happy looking customer who looks exactly like me. We get a nice sleek shot of the car as I drive out of the dealership. The voiceover begins; "At Olaffson our work doesn't stop after your purchase." The car swings out into the street and the John-a-like follows alongside still waving. Cut back inside the car; "Yes, thank you ...yes thanks...goodbye " I say, but John is still hobbling alongside even though it's now starting to speed up. The voiceover resumes; "Our aftercare programme ensures that you have a personal relationship with one of our staff who can help you with any questions that might arise." In my role as the driver I wave goodbye to John, in his role as the dealer and push the gear-stick forward. There's a close-up of my foot stepping on the gas before we cut to a close-up of the speedometer indicating twenty-five mph. He's still out there. He's under pressure but he's still there. Cut to a close-up of Jason's tie caught in the door. The car brakes suddenly. There are embarrassed apologies back and forth. Olaffson. We go further. Shuddering over me Yvette leaned forward and exhaled in my ear.

"Ohhhhhh oui…ouiiiiii."

I would have been very happy to go back to sleep but now I was owed an orgasm. Declining her offer would be regarded as a callous misstep and would require a more carefully worded explanation than I was capable of delivering at four in the morning. It would be wiser to accept her manual advances. She had become very skilled in this department so I knew it wouldn't take long and I'd make sure my gratitude was audible. The next day I was due to become a certified New Yorker. Not because my green card was about to come through, God forbid that should ever materialise, but because on Yvette's insistence, I would start seeing a therapist.

Dr. Jessica Feldman

I told myself that I'd be more open with a woman but the real reason I chose her had more to do with the fact that I could fantasise about fucking her. I already had a story in mind that would, I felt, set the tone for our sessions. It was a story that touched on many of the areas I felt were pertinent to my case and it would give her succinct overview of where I was coming from. A girlfriend invites her man to share his deepest darkest fantasies. He is reluctant at first since deep dark fantasies are often best kept that way, but his girlfriend, intent on getting to know him better, assures him that no matter what he says she won't be shocked because after all it's just a fantasy. Falteringly he begins tell her about how he'd like to be gang-raped. By Japanese schoolgirls. Wearing strap-ons.

She nods understandingly.

"Now you, what's your fantasy?"

It's her turn to be reluctant.

"No. It's too out there."

"Come on, I told you mine"

"Ok, to get married and have kids"

Yvette was simply not willing to continue seeing me until I dealt with my intimacy issues. Fearing an impending sexual embargo I agreed. I wouldn't have even entertained such pusswhippery if she wasn't so sexually adept and in certain lights and on certain days and in her own way, quite beautiful in a non-conventional sort of way.

When she turned up looking terrible I'd feel a jolt of shame as if somehow it was my fault and carefully disguise the emerging grimace under a smile. And on the rare occasion she arrived looking carefree and beautiful like a happy pretty sixteen year-old I'd stifle my glee. The idea being, that either way I was expressionless.

Yes, I was looking forward to therapy.

Dr. Jessica looked directly at my crotch and played with her hair as I talked. She was tall and thin and big-titted and always wore sensible grey skirts and jackets with shiny broaches and sometimes blindingly white blouses over those lovely bulging...oh to do her. The knowledge that every-thing would need to take place within the allotted hour only heightened my fervour.

"So, how was your week?" she'd say.

"Fuck my week." I'd say.

"Fuck me weak." she'd say.

I'd fold her over that big beige armchair and talk about my fantasies of fucking her while I fucked her. That would be worth three hundred and fifty dollars a week at eight o'clock every Wednesday and she wouldn't have to worry about cancellations. But as she creased her smooth buttery forehead in my honour I could sense her willingness not just to witness my pain but to inhabit it. Between imaginary bouts of being butt-fucked, cock-spanked and ass-tongued she somehow managed to point out links I hadn't realised were there. For instance, it was natural she said, that having used a safety pin to prevent Father Teddy from fondling my pre-adolescent balls, I should seek out similar solutions with anyone else who tried to get in.

Maybe my desire to butt-fuck, cock-spank and ass-tongue was an example of this. Perceiving her thus would keep even my therapist at bay. Why was I so distant? She asked me to bring in the recently written ending to what I kept referring to as *my book*. I couldn't see how any of it related to our therapy sessions but because I hadn't shown it to anyone else I thought I might as well get some feedback since she was already on my payroll and so in our next session after reading the last thirty pages of what would eventually become the ending of Diary Of An Oxygen Thief, my therapist confidently proclaimed I was suffering from post-traumatic stress disorder. At least she didn't say it was badly written.

Yvette opened the door to her apartment before I got the key in it.

"I look like shit." she said.

The idea being that because she knew she looked like shit she was relieved of any responsibility for it. If anything, it became my problem since I was now expected to make her feel better about it. Whenever she kissed me her hand would automatically stray to my dick to monitor my affection for her. She hated when I got hard without her knowledge. And that night for some reason maybe because I'd spent the previous hour being investigated or perhaps it was because she did indeed look like shit there was nothing stirring.

"You're not affectionate."

"But your stomach is hurting, I didn't want to..."

"You're distant."

It was a question of theft. There was no hard-on where a hard-on should be. Ordinarily it wouldn't have been a problem. If anything, I was as surprised as she was. The long silence that followed was punctuated by the sighs of a martyr and the whipping back and forth of glossy magazine pages until at last she slipped wordlessly away to bed. I grabbed a pillow and a blanket and made for the couch.

The next morning I was woken by the sound of spigots being turned on and off until finally she appeared in the living room in her uptight formal bank attire looking pinched-face, unfucked and even uglier than the night before. Pausing at the door she turned to look at me on the couch.

"You can go back to bed now." she said.

I was lying on a smouldering hard-on.

*****

Paedophile clergy, punishment-beatings, mental and physical abuse, domestic violence, two near-drownings and the recurring nightmares of the little boy I saw mangled in a farm accident.

"You had a brutal childhood."

Dr. Jessica looked directly into my eyes making sure I heard her. There, it was official. But none of it felt like it had happened to me. I was detached from these events. Had she confused my case with someone else? Maybe she was exaggerating my trauma so I'd keep coming every week. I was after all, her misery-mortgage. And yet I began to enjoy our sessions mostly because it was becoming clear I wouldn't be expected to marry Yvette. That I wasn't so much in love with her, as terrified of letting her down. I was about to marry her out of politeness. Why do that to myself? Or to her? She had her own agenda and her own time-frame. At thirty-three her body-clock was sounding the alarm. I told Dr Jessica about an unusually calm stretch of water on the Niagra River called The Deadline. Once passed there was no way to avoid the pull of the falls three miles ahead. Without looking up from her lap Dr. Susie asked a seemingly unrelated question.

"Have you ever tried online dating?"

*****

Yvette's recently becalmed hell-raising father, was separated but not yet divorced from her artist-mother who for some reason, liked to argue in airports. Her ridiculously handsome brother was a geologist and in a way, so was her privately-educated sister, being as she was, a professional gold-digger. The grandfather on her mother's side made a fortune producing champagne bottles and lived in a small compact stone edifice that could without irony be referred to as a castle. The other grandfather was a retired judge in the French Judiciary with a Parisian street named after him. Rue Du Honore Gumont- Sutre. He owned a summer-house in Ille St Therese where they holidayed at the slightest provocation. Yvette had been abandoned in her fair share of airports and when she wasn't waiting in the lost and found she was watching Papa chase Maman around their antique-laden Parisian home with a kitchen knife.

Her therapist forbade her from telling me too much about her upbringing presumably because she thought I'd be shocked but she couldn't know that having experienced certain childhood eccentricities of my own these nursery tales had a certain soothing effect on me. Anyway, by the time I was formally introduced to Maman I was very well-disposed towards the mass of neuroses, complexes, impulses and moods that stood now collectively before me.

"Bonjour I'm Veronique. It's so nice to meet you"

With her aquiline profile, long dark hair and red leathery skin she looked more like a Cherokee Warrior than the mother of a systems analyst from the Bank of Paris. I had already heard about the legendary debates with airport staff, the aborted attempts to liberate cute little pigs from zoo enclosures and the commandeering of microphones from singers considered unworthy of the title. She bent almost in half to kiss me.

Veronique was an artist. A pretty good one actually. If I hadn't been so consistently afraid of being fired I might have even bought one of her paintings which to my eye, were heavily influenced by Henri Rousseau. I didn't dare tell her that though.

We were en route, en famille to the Metropolitan Museum Of Art to see an exhibition of paintings by Gauguin, because logically enough, he was one of Veronique's favorite painters.

Yvette, though nervous about this meeting was pleased it was happening. She had wanted us to meet at Thanksgiving but this idea had proved too much for me loaded as it was with so much significance. I knew that meeting the parents, or even one of them, at Thanksgiving was tantamount to a marriage proposal. Even if the celebrants were French and Irish there was still an unspoken implication that I was agreeing to something other than just a plate of turkey. But I was ok with Primitivism.

In fact Gauguin was a hero of mine too, since he'd given up his job as a bank clerk to shag French Polynesian girls. Confronted suddenly by an almost life-sized sepia photo of the artist's tight-faced wife and children I felt like I myself had just arrived home late and what time did I call this and who were these two women I'd brought home with me?

"Can't blame him for leaving." I said, and immediately regretted it. It was exactly the wrong thing to say, touching as it, did on Yvette's sensitivity about being abandoned. I braced myself for the public humiliation that would surely follow. I myself was about to become an exhibit.

"Ahh she is so afraid of being abandoned, no?" said Veronique bending even deeper now to kiss her daughter. Yvette's cheeks beamed embarrassment outward into the exhibition space and I suddenly realized Maman was Papa too. She had to be, because Papa had fucked off. But Gauguin had fucked off and they called him a genius. He can't have been the most considerate of men to dump his wife and kids and take off with Van Gogh, that other famous family man. But the Swedish wife took the children to live with her wealthy parents so there was no need to dwell on them too much and they did look pretty fucking boring compared to the technicolor windows into paradise on the walls ahead. I refused to believe that he wasn't fucking every little Polynesian trollop he could get his hands on. Painting all day between orgasms and shagging all night between paintings. Art historians count him amongst the most notable Post-Impressionists but to me his most significant achievement was that he lived in an aftershave commercial before aftershave existed.

"You have found she can be difficult, no?"

We were on the roof patio of the Met Museum and Veronique was talking about her daughter as if she wasn't standing next to her. I mimicked a man testing the ground with his foot and then leaned back in mock-horror as an imaginary explosion leapt from the tiled surface of the roof garden. Veronique smiling eyes met mine and we turned to enjoy Yvette's confusion. The moment felt good and strangely just. This was my cue to produce the glossy book of Gauguin prints from my shoulder bag and hand it to Veronique.

"Pour toi Maman."

I had been forewarned that she loathed people who tried to speak French to her but I had spent a hundred and eighty dollars on the book so I wanted my money's worth. Inhaling loudly and ooh-la-la-la'ing she bowed to kiss both my cheeks again. Real full-on wet kisses not make-up-saving facsimiles.

Wiping my face like I was a rascal she stepped back to regard me. Later, back in her apartment Yvette put away her phone after a long muffled conversation in high speed French. The verdict was in.

"Maman says she thought you loved me passionately and that it was clear to her we would be married. She also said that she herself liked you very much and that you were of superior intelligence."

But then she went on to say that her mother's boyfriend was using the fact that she was too old to have children as an excuse to end their relationship. He was thirty-nine (same age as me) and she was forty-nine. Mother and daughter now shared the same fear of abandonment. Yvette was worried that Maman was on the prowl. It was true she flirted with me but I just assumed this was what French mothers did. She said I would look great in an ornate suit of armor that had been commissioned by the wife of an Austrian count. The sexual possibilities of being the filling in a mother and daughter sandwich were not lost on me but I couldn't suppress the thought that her clit was at least as big as my dick.

*****

"Dare to be average." said Dr. Jessica.

Dare to give me a fucking break.

If I succeeded in being any more average the likelihood of her getting three hundred and fifty dollars an hour would diminish somewhat. We had agreed that I would write down my dreams and so when she asked me if I had anything for her I took out my notebook and read her the following scenario; "I'm setting out chairs in the gym for my Sunday night AA meeting when I become suddenly conscious of making too much noise. I look around and there, between the stacks of chairs are at least seven or eight young boys arranged in sleeping bags on the floor. It's a strange sight but I assume for some reason that they are a junior basketball team who made bad travel arrangements and need somewhere to sleep. As I continue putting out the chairs they begin to wake up and without speaking they stand up and bunch together by the wall waiting for me to finish. This is when I notice they have no arms. I wonder how their vests can possibly remain in place on those smooth rounded shoulders. And because they are well-behaved and respectful it somehow feels ok to introduce them to some of the AA members who by this time are starting to arrive I feel proud of these boys even though I have no idea who they are.

"That's so beautiful, can you see what it is?"

I stared at her.

"Your sub-conscious is telling you it's ok now to bring your younger self into the AA meetings. The boys have no arms because that's how you felt when that guy was touching you."

The boy was contacting the man.

Later that night Yvette called me an asshole with such conviction I almost felt grateful to hear such an honest utterance. Advertising had all but gutted me of any genuine emotion. We had been talking about us. Or rather she had been talking about us while I stewed.

"Do you want to be that guy who has to change his girlfriend every three years?"

Silence.

"Because they'll all want the same thing."

Silence.

Every three years didn't sound so bad to me. If anything, it was a little optimistic.I prayed that I might be struck in love with her. She was after all a ready-made wife, highly cultured, French, great in bed, (if not a little demanding) her mother was an aristocrat and an artist and so well-connected in France I could already see the dappled summers in Belle Ille, the publishing deals in Paris and the French-speaking children showing me the contents of their mouths. But even as I tried to sell it to myself I couldn't conjure the required flutter in my chest. Or if I did it was more like a twitch. Yes, the sex was the best I'd ever had. No doubt about it. Guiltless soaring orgasms that felt like time-travel. So what was wrong? Other girls I'd met were boring in comparison or older or uglier or worse; American. Was I was in denial? Would I only find out how deeply embedded I was when I tried to pull out?

I could think more clearly when we hadn't had sex. In the time we'd been together the orgasms were so intense and so regular they'd had the same effect as medication. Once every two days after meals; and depending on the dosage-level I'd see Yvette as gentle, beautiful and kind and myself as loving, caring and truthful. But now that she was on sexual strike I couldn't find this girl or that guy. Maybe lust was all I'd ever felt for her. There was no point in making us both miserable just because she wanted to have a child. I knew I'd find it impossible to love a creature whose first act on entering the world would be to demolish the one thing I really did have genuine feelings for. Her ass.

Open on a classroom full of boys supervised by a Christian Brother. He walks between the desks craning his head to read the copybooks and pauses to point things out. He stops next to a ginger-haired boy and slides in beside him. The other boys exchange amused looks. Beneath the desk in a close-up shot we see the clergyman's hand emerge from a pocket slit in the side of his gown and crab-creep towards the boy's crotch. The forefinger and thumb pull at the fly fastener on the boy's pants but it doesn't budge. He tries again. Nothing. After one more tug we notice the boy's zipper is pierced by a safety pin.

Cut to a close-up of the boy's face as he allows himself a barely perceptible smile. Match-dissolve to the same boy now wearing an outrageous punk outfit complete with a daisy chain of safety pins from his ear to cheek. The music returns at full volume; "I am an Anti-Christ." The boy gives the finger to camera. Multi-Pack of Xtra-Strong Safety Pins from Boyles Chemist.

Browsing menus of single willing women was intoxicating at first. Pornographic even. Beautiful girls with cocked heads and laughing eyes competing for my attention in a modern day harem. I toiled over half-written messages and deleted them in disgust only to start anew. Finally after agonising over every comma, period and apostrophe I'd send one out like a dove into the night. Annette87 was absolutely gorgeous but believe it or not it was not her beauty that caught my attention. She listed Francis Bacon, a contemporary of Shakespeare, in her *last great book I read* section and for *which superpower would you most like to possess* she'd answered "I'd like to read minds."

So yes, I wrote her a poem.

Look ye to these blackened leaves,
Deathly froze 'neath icy screen,
Neglected thus by suns and moons,
These worried words seek news of you,
Thine eyes to them are planets bright,
Whose orbit brings the gift of life,
Sayest not thou art bereft of powers sublime,
Thou canst read words and therefore minds.

No reply. Maybe she never received it. Should I send it again? Maybe the internet was down. In many ways a fleeting glimpse of a beautiful girl in the street was more merciful. You saw her and she was gone. Here you could ogle what you couldn't have for days on end. Meanwhile capitalising on your disappointment, ads for cars, aftershave and clothes promised to make you more attractive. But I wasn't about to give up.

Intelligence, height, wealth and wit.

These were the most commonly sought qualities on datemedotcom. I already had three of them and I could mimic the fourth in the right shoes. I was never going to attract many replies on my looks alone but I was confident that most girls were going to at least feign interest in a guy who made two hundred thousand dollars a year as an Advertising Art Director. And as such, having worked with some of best digital retouchers in the business I couldn't help but notice that many of the photos had been modified. Skin lightened, blemishes blended, legs lengthened, weight reduced, children removed.

It quickly became clear, after only a few dates, that if a seemingly gorgeous twenty-five-year old girl was willing to meet a guy nearing forty, it meant he was going to have to pull up an extra chair for her ass. Witnessing a girl rearrange the table in front of her as she waited for her anatomical entourage to catch up was not something I wanted to repeat. I felt like the victim of a crime but with no emergency number to call because legislation had yet to catch up with whatever this was.

Scrutinizing the profile photos even more carefully I realized to my horror I had been deceived by three very basic methods of in-camera trompe l'oeil. (1) Lying face-down on a plush carpet absorbed all manner of immensity. (2) Holding the camera high created a false perspective that funnelled even the most amoebic madness into a neat vanishing point. (3) Posing between two friends converted a milk-churn silhouette into an hourglass figure.

I was looking at this all wrong. Instead of being the customer, I needed to become the product. Instead of buying I would sell. At first I didn't catch the significance of profile names like Erin76, Shannon12 and Colleen111, but it soon arrived in me like a smile. As a walking, talking, realistically rendered, three-dimensional, life-sized export of that mythical faraway land called Ireland I had something to sell after all. These misinformed females, having grown up with stories of the old country strained through generations of omission and embellishment, were ripe for the romantic advances of a native-born Mick.

An Irishman with a girl's name?
Yes, that's going to be my headline for this email. You probably get a lot of messages... (gorgeous girl like you) and as you trawl through them going DELETE...DELETE...DELETE.... I thought I'd at least grab your attention with an eye-catching line. ....and let's face it, it must have worked because you're still reading. But why would my parents give me a girl's name? Well, since they had me late in life they knew I'd grow up with less attention than my siblings, and like the Johnny Cash song, A Boy Named Sue, the hope was that I'd grow up independent and tough (imagine the playground taunts). Did it work? You can judge for yourself when we meet.
Girlsname

At first I only copied and pasted this message to girls who referenced Ireland in their profiles but pretty soon I began to send it out randomly. Why not? Irishness was attractive to all cultures except the British and there weren't too many of them over here. And anyway I could always screen the responses later. The objective was to see just what kind of quality I could attract. It was revealing how grateful they all were, beautiful or not, for being referred to as gorgeous. Seemingly, this was enough to blind them to the fact that what they had received was a form letter. And almost all of them wanted to meet, or at least learn more about the man behind it.

"You have two new messages. First message."

Beep.

"I hate you, I hate you, I hate you, I hate you, I hate you, I hate you..." This continued, with a few breaks for inhalation, until the tape ran out.

"New message."

"I hate you, I hate you, I hate you...."

Yvette had obviously felt a need to underline the passion of the first message with the comparative composure of the second. Why was she so aroused? Talking on the phone earlier I had made the mistake of mentioning Dr Jessica's suggestion that I might want to think about online dating and she immediately hung up. Which was just as well because I was about to remind her that it was she who insisted I see a therapist in the first place. If it hadn't been for her I would never have even considered online dating. But when she called back I let the call go to voicemail. Twice. When I felt an urge to call her back I listened to those messages. They were my audible equivalent of a fat-person-picture on a fridge.

Dr. Jessica said I saw conspiracy everywhere.

"Whenever you're stressed or overworked you look around for the enemy. That's your pattern. You learned it from childhood; abuse from your teacher, denial from your mother and now you're doing the same thing with this guy Andy."

Andy was the creative director on Olaffson who very rarely left the building. It seemed to me that if you were any good at what you did you should be able to go home every now and then. But not Andy.

On weekdays we worked into the early hours and on weekends we just worked late. He needed me there because of my experience writing tv commercials and yes I had a better showreel than him but was there really any need for us both to be there at 1am on a Friday night? He tried to make it seem like we were goodpals hanging out together. Just two guys checking out chicks.

"Look at that ass..." he'd say as one of the junior account girls walked by, "...look at the swagger, it's innate."

"It's a nine." I said.

He shook his head in awe.

"That's why they pay you the big bucks."

I'd actually misheard him but he didn't need to know that. That was when I saw through him. Why go home to a complaining wife and screaming kids when you could hang out in trendy office with gorgeous account girls and your witty Irish art director? I was his creative butler.

When I assured Dr Jessica I welcomed the idea of being fired she sighed loudly.

"I'm sorry. You're stuck."

This new candour amazed me. Was it some sort of technique used by therapists? Remain silent for the first five sessions then open up with all sorts of observations? And by encouraging me to remain employed was she thinking not just of my job but her own? I was after all, her misery-mortgage.

"You look smaller this time, last time you seemed taller, you stood more erect, you had greater presence."

This wasn't at all like her. Ordinarily she was

much more tactful about making comments of any kind. I didn't have the heart to tell her that last time I'd worn my Brothel Creepers. They add at least an inch to my height. I was sparing my therapist's feelings now? This was the equivalent of neatening the apartment before the cleaner arrived. Something was wrong. When I first lowered myself into the chair at the beginning of that session the cushion and arm-rests were scorching hot. Re-evaluating my near-collision with a huge mannish-looking woman in the hallway I couldn't help but wonder if I had inherited some of the mood from the previous session.

"Look." she said, shuffling forward in her seat. "What do you do when you come to a fork in the road?"

Was I expected to answer?

"Take it." she said.

I was paying three hundred and fifty dollars an hour for this? Previously, she had appeared all the more intelligent because she had said so little.

BRIDGIT

Bridgit's invitation to inspect the Celtic pendant around her neck allowed me to touch her cleavage which ignited the kiss that led to her bed where, in the throes of fucking her, I noticed a picture of her dad on the bedside table..

He looked exactly like me. My thin-lipped and blue-eyed head lurched forward to fit perfectly over his before retreating and reappearing.

Still a novice, not just to online dating but to dating in general, I agreed to meet her mother who lived in Syracuse. After an exhilarating train ride where she made me come under a newspaper, right there in the seat as the pylons rushed past, I pretended not to notice her mother's expression of euphoria when wide-eyed and hungry for her returned husband, she welcomed me into her house.

I sat at the head of the kitchen table with Nuala, the younger sister, on my left Bridgit on my right. Mom sat at the other end flanked on one side then the other by Paddy the dog. On the wall, a portrait of dad looked down on us from within a gold-frame. He also looked down from the fridge, the hallway, and even from a picture in the toilet where at one point I sought refuge. There was no escaping it.

I was dad.

Bridgit became spokesperson.

"Ok so what do you think of Nuala's progress? Is she heading in the right direction?"

"She still has a few years to fuck around" I said. This was met with squeals of delight.

"And the dog?

"Looks fine to me."

"And what about Mom?"

"I'd do her."

Hysterical laughter punctuated by hand claps. Bridgit respectfully requested that I remove my profile from datemedotcom and I respectfully implied that I might like to keep it up and that was pretty much that until we met again two years later.

*****

In what turned out to be my penultimate therapy session I found myself telling Dr. Jessica that everything had improved, that my fear of intimacy was obviously due to my paranoia and that my paranoia was a result of being abused and that yes, it was still there but I was now able to recognize it for the burden it was, as opposed to the good counsel I had imagined it to be. I acknowledged that as a kid I had drawn a map that had reflected the world around me and that it had been a very useful navigation tool at that time. But now thirty years later I was still using it and wondering why I was bumping into things that according to my map shouldn't be there.

I heard myself acknowledge the success of the sessions while indicating a desire to end them. I shared my vision of a therapy-free existence where it was possible to be well-adjusted without a weekly outpouring of neuroses and cash. I told her, perhaps too honestly, that I spent the intervening days thinking about what to say in the next session so that we wouldn't both have to endure the excruciating silences and shifting-in-seats. And then in an ill-fated attempt at alleviating the timbre of the room I submitted a work-in-progress-tag-line that would work well on small-scale media like fridge-magnets and bumper stickers. I paused for effect.

"Therapy? Enough said."

She smiled at this.

"You wouldn't stop going to AA would you?

Predictably enough, she began to suggest that I might want to continue with the sessions precisely because they were working. I immediately felt uncomfortable. Guilty even. Like I was suddenly extricating myself from a relationship. I waited for her to say I was avoiding intimacy. That I was being distant. That she hated me. I didn't want to continue seeing a therapist when I was already going to a minimum of four AA meetings a week and anyway I felt that what I'd gotten from her was about all there was to get. And let's not forget I already had a sponsor. I did have to admit though, but not to her, that I could see the logic of continuing the sessions since they would at least provide me with someone to bounce ideas off. Someone who could prevent me from making a mistake. Like discontinuing therapy.

NORA

After agreeing to meet Nora on the steps of a church on Eighteenth Street I was amazed when she led me inside to attend a mass that was just starting. Imagining all manner of pagan possibilities I was happy to oblige. But once inside the cavernous candle-lit interior it quickly became clear that six o'clock mass was a gay singles scene where well-dressed young men eyed each other up between the Benediction and the Consecration. My father would sooner die than live in a world where this could happen. In fact, that's exactly what he did.

But Nora didn't seem to notice. She was there to imitate her version of an Irishwoman. To her it was just a look, like Cowgirl or Gypsy. An excuse to wear tweed. She was in a Catholic church with figures kneeling and standing and that was enough for her. It was Ireland by Tommy Hilfiger. Apparently she had gone on a few dates with some guy called Ray. It was pretty clear he hadn't fucked her yet but she mentioned his name often enough that it was clear she wanted to see how I'd address my competitor. This was more of her Irish posturing. I needed to win her. If she hadn't been so pretty I wouldn't have bothered. I emailed her that night.

On the west coast of Ireland, in a city called Limerick, in the shadow of King John's Castle, a black leafless tree inclines itself towards the ochre glow of a streetlamp. In the absence of any natural source of light this gnarled trembling hand reaches for the nearest manufactured equivalent. To imagine so natural a yearning squandered on so cheap a facsimile is too heartbreaking to contemplate so instead dear Nora let us turn our attention to the future. Yours and mine.

xoxo (ps to help you adjust to the imminent glare we might need to get you some Ray-bans)

When I did eventually get her clothes off she was so pale she looked like a corpse. And she pretty much behaved like one. She lay there looking up at the ceiling as if she hadn't noticed I was about to fuck her. I thought about coming on her face just to see her expression but since she had obviously gone to all the trouble of waxing either side of her jet black bush I thought I might as well go down on her. Pretty soon she wouldn't shut up.

"Thank God. Thanks be to Jesus. Oh, thank God!"

It was as if she had misheard the instructions. *Oh Jesus* or *Oh my God* was fine but thanks *be* to Jesus was just frightening. I felt the sting of her juices on my just-shaved face.

"Oh poor thing." she said, "Don't worry, I never come. It's the anti-depressants."

SHEELA
Viewed from the front Sheela was aristocratic

looking, but as soon as she turned even slightly sideways there was a dizzying moment of re-focus while her nose announced its dimensions. Not unlike an aerial view of a ship's mast. She had lovely, clean, pale skin (her parents were Irish), and a beautiful, compact little ass. Tragically though, her hips protruded like a concentration camp survivor. Was I after a relationship or a few fucks? This was a constant source of concern for her. She was looking for chemistry. I was looking for biology. She smiled dreamily into baby carriages while I winced at the back of her head. It occurred to me that had her nose been any bigger and my dick any smaller a blowjob would have been impossible. In the end it was academic. I knew we were finished after a particularly frustrating session trying to keep up with her breathless directions on how to fuck her. She eventually came very loudly, but far from the audible reward I had hoped for I was sure I heard her say "Blaahhhhhh…blah." It summed up our time together.

FRANCESKA

I decided I would never see her again before she even sat down. Her profile picture showed a beautiful girl in a white t-shirt and high heels taking her own photo in a full length mirror. The scenario had a Helmut Newtonish feel to it and I assumed this was why she had used the old Leica to capture it. A witty prop for a tongue-in-cheek shoot. Having described herself as a hybrid photographer-assistant-model-writer it made sense to present herself in this way. It also made perfect sense to meet her for a coffee. But as she approached I realised her decision to use a Leica was more than just a retro-chic affectation. It was a mask. A digital camera would have required her to hold it away from that face. She was a hybrid alright. The world-weary head of an Irish politician surveyed the cafe from the body of a lingerie model.

"I'm so sorry." she said.

I tried not to stare."...for being late. I couldn't find the place, I almost walked past."

"Don't worry, you're worth the wait." A lie so enormous a car probably crashed somewhere.

"Thank you..." she said reaching into her bag. "You don't look anything like your picture."

I hid my rage as she took out a small black wallet and began to show me badly composed photographs printed on cheap paper. Even if she had been stunningly beautiful I would have been unhappy about this, but under the circumstances I was breathless.

"Really?"

While she talked, mostly about her photography, I tried to summon a version of myself that could somehow ignore her from the neck up, or more precisely from the chin up, because there was something there casting a small shadow. I couldn't quite tell what it was and though I wanted to study it, I didn't dare.

"Do you still want to meet in Ireland?"

She didn't actually have any Irish heritage but because she loved everything about the country I had talked about a romantic rendezvous in Deelford. I hadn't told her I was already due there the following week for a visit home because I had wanted to make it seem like I was planning the trip around her.

But that was before we'd met.

"Yes" I said involuntarily and threw in a nod to make it more believable.

"Yes? But it's very expensive, no?"

Was she was offering me an escape or was she trying to get out of it herself? Or was she pretending she didn't fancy me so I wouldn't feel obligated? Or was she angling for a free flight? I couldn't read that face one way or another. The fact that she could use a camera to hide her face might well have been the reason she got into photography in the first place. There was an ad for cameras in there somewhere. You get more detail with a digital camera. I tried to summon a version of myself that could somehow see it as a large pimple. A chin-nipple perhaps, but it was useless. The wart wagged the woman.

MOTHER

After an overnight flight to Dublin and a joyless train ride to Deelford I was jolted from a virtual sleepwalk into the kitchen of my childhood home to find my brother and mother touching my jacket like Bangkok peasants. It would not have seemed surreal if I thrown coins to the floor. Only slightly more dignified I placed a fifty-Euro note between the salt cellar and the sauce bottle and emptied my caressed coat-pocket of coins into my mother's wide expectant hands. This secured my first compliment.

"Doesn't he look great?"

This was the Ireland I remembered.

Before I'd even sat down she warned me not to call the fire brigade since the last time I was home I had needed their services to extinguish a chimney fire. Having recently taken to counting each separate rock of coal my mother was hardly going to welcome the cost of having the chimney swept. The last time already mindful of her sensibilities I had very carefully placed one diamond-in-waiting on what appeared was no more than a pathetic sputtering flame but apparently the chimney couldn't deal with the increased traffic and the smoke began to back up. I had no idea the fire brigade charged by the hour. I thought they were a government service like the postman or the police.

My laptop was met with oohs and awws.

My mother began to drop the first of many hints that she needed to pay off one thousand Euros on a car accident she'd caused. She left a silence after this which I suppose, I was expected to fill with money but when I pretended not to understand she stopped making me cups of tea. Brian said I was paranoid about my money, that I was obsessed with it.

"I'm not the one obsessed with it." I said

There was another silence after that.

Due to the prohibitive cost of oil the central heating was never on for more than an hour a day even in December. Brian had discovered that sleeping with a pair of underpants over his head afforded the warmth of a hat but with more ventilation. He helpfully began to explain that seventy percent of your body heat escaped through your head. He had obviously forgotten that it was I who told him this after serving two years of my life in Minnesota. I wanted to suggest he'd be even warmer if he shut his fucking mouth, but I didn't. I pitied him living in that house with that woman.

She was really pissed off that her husband was

dead. She couldn't see that she was in fact very lucky to have someone, anyone, at home with her, even if it was only Brian. The house had gotten worse since dad died. There were pockets of unwiped goo everywhere. It was all too familiar and yet it was like some sort of dream. Brian without his wife and my mother without her husband. They'd become a sort of sexless bickering couple and I was the umpire. In the mornings I'd hear them stiffly descending the creaking stairs. The undead.

I gave my mother a signed copy of The Potter And The Petal and joked that it would be would be worth a fortune some day because it was a hardback and the author was quite reclusive. She was happy about this until she noticed my inscription wishing her a Happy Christmas. I had obviously devalued it. I looked past her annoyance, like I had done so many times before out the kitchen window at the black defeated trees and I felt fortunate I could leave. When she got sad about me leaving I was reminded of all the times I'd left home for Art College in Limerick or London or St LaCroix or New York. My tears became easier and easier to hide until there were none.

My constant state of sleeplessness was like some sort of torture technique where my eyes were sewn open and I was forced to watch something I didn't want to see. My mother's decline and my brother's misery.

I rose early the next morning after another sleepless night. I crept quietly around the kitchen so as not to wake them. The less conversation the better. There were only two more days before I flew to Las Vegas but I desperately tried to think of excuses to leave earlier. I was in exactly the same place I'd sat when I first told my mother about Brother Ollie thirty years earlier. I remember waiting as she drained yellowish green water from a saucepan of boiled cabbage. I was about to inform on the coolest priest at my school. At nine years of age I couldn't even be sure that what I was about to tell my mother was controversial. Mostly I was looking for a reaction. Shock. Disbelief. Laughter. For all I knew I might have been leading the priest astray. After all, why would a man dedicated to God want to play with the thing I peed with? The only satisfactory explanation was that I was evil. Some weeks after I had established the habit of going to school with my trusty safety pin in place I experienced what I would later realise was a sexual stirring. As Brother Ollie approached preceded by the smell of his hair cream and aftershave I actually wanted him to come and sit beside me, to touch me, down there. I even removed the safety pin, just in case. This means that my very first sexual yearning was not only co-opted by the Catholic Church, it was rejected. But the cabbage was more important.

"Oh," she said, "he's just being friendly."

She dissolved as the steam enveloped her. I was her fifth Caesarian in a row. She barely had time to heal between births. It must have been difficult for the surgeon to find fresh skin for his blade. Each of us literally left a huge scar on her. Mid-century Ireland was a moral-middle ages where Priests, Nuns, Brothers and Bishops were feared like Gestapo and contraception was the stuff of science fiction. The way things were back then she was lucky she didn't have four more children.

So were they.

Open on a rainy farmyard somewhere in Ireland. A potato grader juts out of a barn as underage workers try to keep pace with the conveyor belts. Cut inside the barn where a young boy pitchforks potatoes into the funnel of a grader as other boys positioned on either side of the machine busy themselves separating rotten specimens from the healthy. They all wear hooded anoraks against the rain and black potato sacks around their waists like makeshift aprons. In a close-up we see the uncovered cog and chain mechanism that powers the conveyor belt and we realise now as we pull back that the boy with the pitchfork is leaning dangerously close to it as he works. Another small figure scurries along in the rain edging past the others as he makes his way towards the boy on the end.

One boy with a shock of ginger hair protruding from his hood (it's the same boy from the safety-pin commercial) notices something strange about the newcomer. His hood is larger and darker than the others and oddly he carries a scaled-down scythe which appears custom-made for his size.

Suddenly the conveyer belt lurches and shudders. Something is jammed in the mechanism. The ginger-haired boy looks in the direction of the upset just in time to see two little legs in swing impossibly into the air and fall away again. The grader continues to lurch and grind until the ginger-haired boy finds the switch. There is no sign of the strange little hooded boy with the scythe. We hear the voiceover say; "Tragedy comes in all sizes so keep protective guards on all moving parts. Issued by the Irish Government for Safety in Agriculture.

My mother's technique for coping with the grief of losing her husband of forty three years was to refuse food in the hope that she might join him. On her way up to bed that night as she carefully closed the living room door so as not to disturb my television viewing, I had the strangest sense that I was seeing her alive for the last time. In stark contrast a memory of her whooping with laughter flashed into my mind. What the fuck did I care about the television? I was only sitting there trying to postpone another sleepless night in my freezing damp bed. An urge to save her suddenly rose within me. I'd bring my energy intelligence, and wit to bear on the situation. I won't let you die ma. Don't worry I'm here. I'll save you. But then I realised I was powerless. I couldn't make her want to live. It was her decision. The living room door was like a coffin-lid closing over her.

"You don't have a vocation, you should start a family." Being sent home from a seminary before you'd taken your final vows was the kind of thing that was whispered about in fifties Ireland where having a priest in the family was better than a relative in government.

But for my dad it was not to be.

The Bishop himself had just ordered my father to go forth and multiply. This was no mere whim it was an ecclesiastical directive. Had he been around today he probably would have signed up for online dating. The speed with which he found the one he wanted seemed to suggest that he might have had his eye on her for some time. Brenda Sullivan was pretty and well-off and promised to another. And it didn't help that her family were aiming higher than a failed priest. So when he received an invitation to her wedding his faith quaked. Not good enough for the priesthood and certainly not good enough for the Sullivans.

"God only breaks your heart so he can get in." he would tell me many years later. The Bishop was God's representative on earth and my father would do his bidding. In wide-shouldered suits that hung vertically from his thin frame and well-spoken after his six years in the seminary he must surely havecut a dash in the countrified dance-halls of downtown Deelford. My mother certainly thought so. She was taken with his manners and poise and of course his looks. He and his two brothers had strong intelligent angular foreheads with brows that sheltered deep-set mostly blue eyes and even in their later years they took turns throwing their heads back in loud uncontrollable guffaws.

All dead now of course. Except for Frank, the youngest at seventy-nine. My mother couldn't bear to let him into the house during those first few weeks following the funeral looking as he did, so much like a skinnier paler version of her dead husband.

He was like a ghost knocking at the door.

Her nickname for Brian was "Flash" precisely because he wasn't. She complained constantly that he couldn't be arsed to find real work and that there fore he was a depressing influence. Divorce seemed like such a glamorous word to use in connection with him because nothing had happened to Brian since well, nothing had ever happened to Brian. He was receiving back-pay from fate. I once walked in on him in the toilet and found him pissing not into the toilet but in the sink. He did this so he could continue watching himself in the mirror. It wasn't vanity so much as self-surveillance. Directly after his divorce he was so bereft of ideas about what to do he was like a life-size doll between positions. Brian making a cup of tea. Brian sitting. Brian standing. Brian walking. Brian sitting again. Talk about teachable. If my mother hadn't managed to fuck him up the first time she was getting a second chance. They very quickly became an eccentric modern couple. Her bringing over fifty years of marital experience to the table and Brian bring nothing at all. He didn't pay rent. Her friends remarked on how closely he resembled my father and how lucky my mother was in effect, to have him back.

But she didn't see it this way. When he drove me to the station on a morning so moist it might have been regurgitated, I was so elated at the prospect of leaving that damp rotting ancient island I almost fell out of the car when it stopped. He mock-saluted and drove away eyeing himself in the re-angled mirrors.

But it wasn't over yet.

From the platform I could see the farm where Timmy was killed. Much was made of the fact that I broke into the farmhouse to call the ambulance. Like it was an act of heroism. But I would have done anything to get away from the image of my friend dangling by the throat with the hood of his duffel coat woven obscenely into his pale skin. Breaking a window was the cowardly thing to do. I should have stayed and helped him. But as it turned out there was no escaping the horror of that day. Turning around with the phone still in my hand I was met by an equally disturbing sight. One of the other boys was busy robbing the place.

As the train pushed the damp empty buildings aside I realised my Christmas had consisted of four freezing days and nights in a damp house with a bitter old woman and a divorced unemployed barman. No wonder I was relieved to get out. I left five hundred Euros on the mantle-piece to ease my guilt. Brian joked that my sister and I should pay him since he was basically running an old folk's home for one. He can't have known that if he had insisted I would have been happy to set up a standing order. I looked up and down the train to see if there were others like me who couldn't wait to leave this wet washed-out, rained-on place. The train was full.

ERIN
Erin a pale red-haired beauty looked out at me from the just opened jpg. She was young. Twenty-nine is young when you're almost forty. I had already fed her email address into Facebook to see if she had a big ass in tow and here she was not as clear-skinned in an un-photoshopped version of the same photo she'd posted on datemedotcom but her body was visible now so that didn't seem to matter. I leered over profile for a while before calling her.

She had been married before she said and now wanted kids. She had a little dog she'd bought from Puppies on Lexington. She was going to a wedding that Saturday and was doing her laundry on Sunday and hiring a car for the weekend. She lived in Nassau and though she loved having sex she was allergic to condoms and so could only do it with a specific condom made from lambskin.

"They're expensive and not easy to get." she said
"How much is expensive?"
"Twenty-five dollars."
"Each?"
"Yep."

There was something refreshing about her lack of finesse. She encouraged me to speak so she could hear my accent. She wanted me. Pure and simple. No games. She invited me to go to the wedding with her that Saturday. It would be a two and half hour drive with and a six-month old puppy on my lap and three hours being paraded around like a captured American serviceman. I was thankful to be able to truthfully tell her I had to be in Las Vegas for work. This impressed her. She was not quite white trash but getting there. Off-White maybe. Eggshell. She bemoaned the fact that she couldn't drink at the wedding since she was driving but she would make up for it the following night. She'd recently had a few one-night stands with a Texan who bought drinks for everyone in the bar wherever he went. She said this kind of behaviour embarrassed her but she couldn't refuse a man who bought her drinks all night. And yes, she had sex with him.

"Did you use a custom-made lambskin condom?"
"Well no, not that night silly, we were, you know,

drunk "

"I like the idea of the lambskin condom because as an Irishman it satisfies my desire to shag sheep and women at the same time"

"I'll pretend I didn't hear that."

"I'll pretend I didn't say it."

Hearing her laugh I imagined her covering our child's ears in her version of our future. Isn't daddy awful? I had a headache after forty minutes of listening to her. I had only stayed that long in the hope that I might step into the toilet for some phone sex. But she was obviously thinking further ahead than I was. She wanted to get into my genes. So when she asked if I had the Orish Curse I pretended not to understand.

"Well yes, I suppose I do. I'm an alcoholic. In fact I've been in AA now for fifteen years." It seemed like as good a way as any to extricate myself.

"Good for you..." she said, obviously winded. "Congrats." And then after a pause, "Fifteen years? Why, how old are you?"

"Forty-eight" I lied.

"Your picture looks a lot younger'.

"That's what happens when you don't drink"

Another pause presumably for calculation.

"So you're seventeen years older than me."

She was audibly disappointed. She had just lost a house in upstate New York, three children, two rabbits and a dog. All I wanted was a wank and that was still possible without her.

Open on a shot of a railway tunnel somewhere

in the Ireland. Birds chirp and bees buzz as the voice-over begins; "At the age of 16 you are legally entitled to two of life's greatest pleasures."

Suddenly a high-speed train thrusts itself into the tunnel and continues to disappear into the small snug-fitting opening. The voiceover resumes with a snicker; "The other one is the Young Person's Railcard."Cut to a still-life shot of the Young Person's Railcard with an id-photo of the same ginger-haired boy we saw in the farmyard commercial earlier. He has grown up a little and now sports ginger sideburns to match.

Irish Rail, How Far Will You Go?

I was so tired after my sleepless week in Ireland all I could remember about Air Lingus flight E1090 to Las Vegas was a very unattractive girl on my left saying there might be empty seats up front and a toddler imitating the sounds of someone being brutally killed on my right. And from behind me unseen knees pressed urgently into the small of my back. I must have passed out because at the moment of landing I jolted awake in a stupor of self-hatred and dissatisfaction in Las Vegas McCarren International Airport.

A small neat Mexican man in a small neat suit waited with a sign on which the word Miss preceded my name. When I pointed at it he just smiled like I was joking and continued scanning the incoming hordes for the real me. I stood there waiting for him to understand. He stepped away. I stepped closer. I was too exhausted to do anything else. It took longer than usual but when he realised his mistake he placed the sign in a nearby trash-can and looked for a moment as if he might get in there with it.

"I'm very sorry, Sir."

Having established my identity he took me in his darkened car to a cultural abattoir known as The Merchant of Venice Hotel where in room 31014, after enduring forty-five minutes of taped messages and bad adsI was so relieved to hear a live human being,I shouted at him. After a half-hearted, half-heard apology I was thrust back into Tele-purgatory. I slammed the phone down in disgust and picked it right back up again. This led to a conversation with my mother who was at that moment watching re-runs of the A Team and I knew without having to be told that I'd have to call her back. Far from wanting to hear my mother's voice I wanted to avenge myself on the agency by running up as big a phone bill as possible.

"It's freezing cats and dogs here." she said when I was at last deemed worthy of an audience.

"What's it like over there?"

But before I could answer she began telling me how Murdoch in the A-Team reminded her of my brother and the rest of the "conversation" was about how sad it was that he couldn't get another woman and what did I think about that. Did I think he'd be able to get a woman on that thing that I did on the computer because after all I seemed to be doing alright by it and I let's face it I was no looker. But again, before I could get a word in she was off again.

"Do you know Mrs O'Shaughnessy?

"No, Ma I don't think so."

"You do, you met her."

"Did I?"

"Angela O'Shaughnessy."

"No, I don't know her."

"Married to Seamus O'Shaughnessy."

"I can't say I know her."

"You do, I'm telling you."

"Where does she live?"

"Cuff's Grange."

"I don't know where that is."

"You do, you do, we were there once."

"Does she have red hair.?"

"No, you bleddy eejet that's Nuala, you said she had to throw her boobs over her shoulder before she could tee off."

"Ahh. Yes. Now I have her yes, what about her?"

"She's dead."

Now I wanted to shout at her too. I actually did a couple of times but my cell phone service provided gaps into which my expletives fell and rendered me civil. Not that she would have noticed, she just kept talking and talking as I paced around the horror that was my room; imitation books fashioned from fibreglass, mass-produced carpets with badly done fleur-de-lis and garish marbling even on the air-conditioners. I had to get out.

The interior was tasteful compared to the outer façade. Standing outside in the blazing sunshine I could see only too clearly now the full-scale formaldehyde replica of St Marks Tower with its digital screen presiding over plastic gondolas ruddered by stocky blonde women in khaki cut-offs. The canals looked like they were filled with blue paint and for all I knew maybe they were.

On that short unforgettable walk to a desperately

needed AA meeting I encountered in this order; a scaled down version of the Eiffel Tower, The Brooklyn Bridge and yes, the Great Pyramids of Egypt. Why visit Paris, New York or Cairo, when you could pose in front of these effigies and save yourself the journey. A digital crawl attached to a skyscraper announced "Paintings By Pablo Picasso....Eduard Manet...Paul Gauguin....and many... many ....more...."

My old friend Gauguin, here?

Seeing the names of these artists presented in the same manner as Tony Bennett got me thinking that it would be great to enclose Las Vegas in a glass dome and present the entire city as a post-modern post-ironic work of art. A geosphere of what-not-to-do. A metropolitan objet trouve.

But this wasn't art. It was life. My life. And I hated my presence in it. I was being swallowed whole by a sort of daylight darkness. This wasn't just a job any more. It was a condition where affection, friendship, honesty, and kindness were co-opted to lever a purchase. I needed an AA meeting. On the way there I called my sponsor and begged him to let me resign.

"Go in till lunch-time tomorrow," he said, "and call me then."

Open on a shot of me at work listening to headphones when suddenly we hear a booming voice. "Sell. Your. Apartment." Maybe I had down-loaded something weird. Probably some creative real-estate commercial aimed at iPad users. I shuffle to the next track.

"Sell. Your. Apartment."

I remove the headphones. Strange. Maybe there's a virus in my computer. I carry on working until lunch-time and just as I'm about to get into the elevator I hear the voice again.

"Sell. Your. Apartment."

I look at the guy in the elevator beside me.

"Did you hear that?

"Hear what?"

"A voice saying, sell your apartment."

He looks like he's disappointed in me. This continues over the next few days. I hear the voice saying the same thing at the most unexpected times; on the toilet; just before going to sleep. Cut to a SOLD sign being taken down outside my apartment.The voice seems to have stopped until...

"Put. The. Money. In. A. Bag."

By now I'm starting to look pale and underslept. In quick cuts I first enter and then exit a bank with a flight-case full of cash. There must be three hundred thousand dollars in there. In the park I take out a hundred dollar bill from the case to buy a sandwich. I'm looking up now waiting for the voice to say something but nothing happens. Some dodgy-looking characters start eyeing me up. I'm getting nervous. Finally, the voice says one word;"Flight." I misunderstand this instruction and I get up and run. I am followed by three sketchy guys who can barely keep up. Cut to an airport departure-screen. "Flight E1090" In a close-up we see I have the matching ticket in my hand. The flight departs for Las Vegas. Clutching the flight case, I fall asleep on the plane. After landing in Las Vegas I step out of the terminal, jump into a cab and wait.

"Where do you…?"

I put one finger to my lips. The cab driver looks at me in the rear view mirror. We wait.

"The. Merchant. Of. Venice." the voice says at last. I relay this to the driver. Arriving outside the hotel I am welcomed by porters and ushered inside. Still clutching the flight case I wander around the hotel lobby sauntering between the roulette tables and slot machines while I wait for instructions. One hugely overweight man in a t-shirt that says In the Zone has fallen asleep in front of a slot machine. I look around desperately. What am I doing here? Maybe I'm losing my mind? I start to cry.

"Third. Table. On. The. Right."

I push through the gamblers till I reach a roulette table surrounded by people already in the middle of a cycle. The ball clatters to a stop and two people walk away dejected leaving a gap in the crowd. I heave the flight case onto the table. This must be it. The moment that will make sense of it all. I open the case and tip the contents onto the baise. A loud groan of pleasure emanates from the onlookers.

"Put. It. All. On. Twenty-Four."

I make an ineffectual attempt at grouping the money into one area as if to ensure it straddles the number twenty-four.

"Red." the voice says.

Accordingly I shove the mound of money a little to the right.

"No more bets."

The croupier is adamant. The wheel is spun. All eyes are on the little metal ball as it revolves inside the roulette wheel for what seems like an eternity.

There is at least four hundred thousand dollars in cash on the table. People saunter over from other tables and a quiet descends as the croupier flashes a look at the security camera overhead. In black and white extreme close-up we see the little metal ball bounce, hop, skip, skidder and wink. At last the wheel slows down and the ball seems to be trying out random compartments for comfort before leaping out to try another. Finally as the spinning subsides the individual compartments move slowly enough to be discernible. The ball sits in a black compartment. Number twelve. A collective groan rises from the spectators and they immediately disperse as if such misfortune is contagious.

"Aww. Shit." the voice says.

The croupier drags the stack of money towards him and begins stuffing it into the slot in the table. A title appears on the screen.

For more reliable investment advice call Belvedere Bank Services 0800 244 7864.

JESSICA

"...now push your hips up to me because I want to shove my stiff cock inside you....but I'm going to make you wait... you'll have to beg me....I want to hear you beg me..." I held the phone to my cock so she could hear it squelching as I pummelled it.

"Can you hear that?"

Silence. She wasn't sure if she should be doing this and yet she wanted me to continue.

"Yes."

"That's what your cunt will sound like when

I fuck it with my stiff cock."

"Ohhhh."

Interesting to note that the word *cock* on its own didn't seem to have any effect until it was accompanied by the word *stiff, hard* or *rigid*. A cock was just a cock but a stiff cock was a compliment. The power of the adjective.

"Ohhhh."

Sometimes I'd experiment and leave long silences inviting the caller to guess what I'd say next (I'd have to resist throwing in something surreal like *lawnmower* or *tupperware* just to see what would happen) These silences would sometimes bring forth surprises.

"I want you to come in my mouth."

The dirty little cunt. She would never have said that if we had just met in Starbucks.

"You're a dirty little cunt." I said

"Ohhhh."

Over the tannoy system the stewardess bade passengers to return to their seats.

"You're on a plane? I've never done it on a plane."

"You have now."

As I left the toilet cubicle I must have looked like I had just received some excellent news. This was better than real sex. I would definitely be calling her again. A jpg arrived in my phone of a picture she'd taken seconds earlier; a close-up of two glistening fingers inside herself. We were approaching New York and I had a date.

DIANE

Diane turned up at Cafe Mozz looking so gorgeous and tiny and cute I wanted to have sex with her there and then in the street against the wall. In her profile, she looked like a ten-year old boy with tits and so I was already a little ashamed of the explicit nature of my intentions towards her before she even turned up. But she seemed to enjoy the attention. Or was it my discomfort? She looked so young a siren went off somewhere inside me.

All her clothes came from the children's section of Old Navy and she had become quite adept at removing cartoon characters and bunny rabbits but sometimes she said she liked to leave them on. There was a pause here as she waited for my reaction. Sometimes she left them on? Why would she tell me that? An unspeakable sexual sea-creature caught the light for a second a slithered silently back into the murk. Such a sighting could never be report- ed. Maybe it was a diversionary tactic designed to sway me form the fact that her interest in me was purely professional. She couldn't mention that what she really wanted was a photo assignment and I couldn't give voice to my illegal longings.

"I love your emails." was the first thing she said to me in person. This of course was clever of her not just because it was flattering but because my emails to her had been predominantly erotic in nature.

Here are my balls,
This is my penis,
My hopes are high,
It'll come between us.

She allowed me to believe that I might have my way with her that very night if it wasn't for the fact that she needed time to get over her ex-boyfriend.

What she didn't mention and what I found out later was that she was already living with a man and would go home to him that very evening. She was very pretty in a pointy sort of way and even though she did her best to behave like a lost little girl in a world of wonder the prominent nipples under the tight white cotton of her skin-tight t-shirt seemed to suggest otherwise. That she had chosen amongst all the clothes in her wardrobe to wear such a revealing t-shirt to our first date gave me a thrill that must have informed my features. I assumed it was one of the items of clothing she had referred to earlier. And since I was the one doing most of the talking the conversation seemed to sparkle. At the end of an excellent evening after a faux argument about who should pay the bill (I won) she jokingly punched the air between us and I angled my cheek mimicking impact. But misreading my intention she leaned forward to kiss me there instead. Suddenly in danger of rejecting a kiss I hadn't expected I clumsily kissed her cheek as she tried to kiss mine. This was particularly dishonest of her since she had effortlessly conjured up one of those awkward romantic moments that so often occur between people still unsure of the others' affections. This seemed like a good time to tell her that I had been working too hard and it would be nice to slow down a little.

"Yes, you should be kinder to yourself" she said, ingratiating herself with someone that could lead to a seventy-thousand-dollar-a-day photo-assignment.

"My first act of self-kindness will be to see you again on Wednesday night" I said camouflaging my desire to rip off her child-sized knickers and fuck what I found there.

"I'd like that." she said, blushing at her own dishonesty.

"Excellent." I said, mortified by mine.

I googled her name and a blog came up featuring the daily trials of a fixer-upper as she renovated a brownstone in Bushwick. There was a picture of her in a check shirt cuddling a huge wild-haired fucker in a newly delivered claw-footed bathtub. "Me And My Man." the caption said. The plumbing alone would cost a fortune.

*****

Back in the agency the following day just before lunchtime I was printing out fifty pages of Diary Of An Oxygen Thief as requested by a potential literary agent when suddenly standing there beside me was Andy. He was waiting for something of his own to print and he just kept turning over my emerging pages and smirking to himself. I couldn't stop him. He was entitled to look for his printout. I couldn't stop the printer either I would have pulled out the plug if I had known were it was.

Click whirr….pffht..

"I liked hurting girls."

Click whirr…pffht…

"Your cunt is loose."

Click whirr…pffht…

"Call that a head-butt?"

Slivers of my life being served like Prosciutto. Eleven pages in the tray meant thirty-nine more to go. Sweet Jesus make it stop.

"So this is your big break-out novel?"

He didn't look up from the pages as he spoke. I shouldn't have been printing anything that wasn't work-related. Before I could answer our account director Perry walked over with some other guy in a suit I'd never seen before. Andy looked quite handsome when he was enjoying himself.

"Do you want me to call you when it's done?"

"No. That's alright, I'll wait. So, do you have a publisher?"

"Not yet, I'm sending this to an agent."

He raised his chin and nodded once as if this explained everything he'd ever wondered about. I decided to hide in the men's room for a few minutes. When I felt enough time had elapsed I'd come out and retrieve my vileness from the printer and retreat to my office and call my sponsor and beg him to let me resign. But after only a few seconds of pretending to piss Andy seemed to spring from the floor at the urinal beside me.

"So, do you have these in Europe?"

He was referring to the flushers on the urinals which might or might not have been particular to the US and I suspected he already knew the answer before he asked me. I turned to look at him mostly in disbelief. Was he going to work in some witty remark about me being flushed down the toilet and never getting another job again? This fucking guy. I pretended to misunderstand.

"Penises? Yeah we have them, but they're much bigger."

The easy smile froze onto his face.

"Remind me not to set you up like that again." he said. Had I lost my mind? This guy had the power to fire me. Without a job I was an illegal immigrant.

Open on a shot of me with my own shoe-shine
stall. A suited executive talks on his cell phone as I
finish giving him a shine. The camera finds my sad
forlorn face in the refection of his shoe. In that same
reflection somebody steps into view behind me. I
look down at the pavement and instead of another
pair of men's shoes I see what appears to be a pair of
ladies high-heeled boots. But as the camera follows
my gaze upwards we realise the girl is wearing a
one-piece leather cat-suit stretched tantalisingly
over every contour of her gorgeous body. And
though she's flawless in every way the leather looks
lacklustre and uncared for. She needs a damn good
buffing.

Keeping her eye on me she gingerly steps up
onto the shoe-shine-stand and dramatically dusts off
the seat before lowering herself into position.
Passers-by stop to look at her. She's that beautiful.
I try to remind myself she's a customer but it's
impossible to hide the effect she's having on me. Is
she naked beneath that body-hugging leather?
Obviously enjoying my discomfort she uncrosses
her legs and offers me a foot. I reach for a piece of
cloth but when I try to spit on it I realise my mouth
has gone dry. Unperturbed she leans provocatively
forward and offers me her bottle of Perrier.

A title appears on the screen.

Perrier. Thirst for Life.

MISS CANADA

But I wasn't fired. I was assigned to oversee yet another shitty commercial, this time being shot in Canada where all five cars in the Olaffson stable demonstrate their snow-traction capabilities as they converge at a ski-lodge for the holidays. Each member of an unlikely family drive a Falfaux and it is only due to this that they can be together for the Holidays. A lesser car would have careered off the road. This, it turned out was the script Andy had been waiting for that day at the printer. And this assignment it turned out was his way of punishing me for being so brazen as to announce my ambitions of being a writer. All advertising creatives have at least one book, musical, screenplay, or children's book hidden under the metaphorical floorboards, but it's considered very bad taste to talk about it. Why talk of escape when you're in a maximum-security prison?

Our freelance producer found some idiot French-Canadian director to shoot it on the cheap because he was as desperate to get into the business as I was to get out of it. Before we even landed in Calgary I couldn't wait to leave. The director, Jean-Philip, asked in his thick French accent if I needed anything shot for my reel. He must have guessed I was so bored with this shoot that he needed to offer something extra to keep my interest.

Creatives often asked directors to shoot personal projects on the back of a fully paid-up production but even if I had something in mind I wouldn't have trusted this guy with it. But he was way ahead of me. Eager to impress, he had already thought of an alternative. That same evening after the so-called shoot, (it was all over after two hours) the client, Ken (No-Ken-Do as I called him), our freelance producer (I forgot his name) and myself were picked up in a huge SUV outside the hotel and taken to Calgary Adult Entertainment Club.

Within seconds of being us shown into the VIP area and offered a drink I didn't want, I realised I had no prior reference for a rabbit-fur bikini.

Why would I? It had never occurred to me that a bikini could be made from such material. It wasn't practical. It contradicted itself. It was like a lamp lit by a candle. But the contrasting textures of fawn coloured fur and the clean white skin almost got me going. I say almost because the lighting was too harsh and the interior too cavernous and let's not forget that getting even a hint of a hard-on in the same room as No-Ken-Do was an imponderable.

"She's a former Miss Canada" the sideways shift of his eyes was all he could afford to confirm that I was indeed there beside him. I could hardly believe it myself as I risked a sideways glance of my own at the leaning tower of red chips surging upwards from his table representing only too graphically his desire for the alarmingly young girl on the stage in front of us. As he lobbed, flicked and tossed these plastic discs, the artist formerly known as Miss Canada positioned herself expertly to catch each filthy thought above her now fur-free and hairless vagina.

This, it turned out was Canada's real attraction. Not the strength of the dollar or the endless available snow but the fact that the strippers were allowed to go nude.

"In Canada the beaver goes free." said Kenneth Berg, Olaffson's recently promoted Marketing

Director who at that moment was busy scrunching up his nose like he was making faces for a baby. But this vagina was dry and uninterested. I knew this because I could see right into it. Its owner made absolutely no attempt to appear aroused by what she was doing and as a result neither did I.

Until later. After refusing the second offer of free drinks I slipped away and hailed a cab back to the hotel where I had a Posh Wank (I used a condom) and fell sideways asleep still clinging to my dick. In a dream, I was reciting a customised version of the right-to-bear-arms-motto; "You'll have to take this dick from my cold dead hands", when I was awoken at three-am by a knock on the door.

"Your early morning call, Sir."

The producer had arranged it because apparently I was due back in the office. And so it came to pass, while boarding that half-understood fateful five-am flight to New York, I was stopped by an immigration officer in Toronto Airport.

"I'm sorry Sir, your visa has expired."

I feigned wakefulness.

"My what is…what?"

The producer was already on the plane. My bags were being recalled. My phone was dead. I remember feeling the beginnings of a Tsumani surge of panic that almost immediately subsided and settled into what could only be described as relief.

Something significant was happening.

My HIB work visa was out of date and there was simply no way in the present politically fraught environment they were going to let me back to New York where, let loose amongst the unsuspecting public I might put the finishing touches to yet another crap commercial. They were right. I had to be stopped.

"So, I can't go back to New York?"

"No Sir. You're staying in Toronto."

Harsh punishment indeed.

I was shown into a windowless room where a huge, testicle-faced man in a blinding white shirt did his best to behave like he was asking trick-questions.

"But you just said you flew in from Calgary."

"Yes."

"So where were you going?

"New York."

"What for?"

"I live there."

"But you have an Irish passport."

"Yes, but I live in New York."

"And you say you were shooting a commercial."

"In Calgary, yes."

"What do you do?"

"I'm an art director."

"What does that entail?"

"Making the copywriter look good."

His eyes remained on my passport.

"And you don't drink?"

"What, no?"

"Nothing at all?"

"No."

"Not even at Christmas?"

"No."

"And you're Irish?"

"Yes, I'm Irish."

"Conas ata tú?"

Were they fucking serious? I was being asked

questions in Gaelic now? And how did he know I didn't drink? Had they looked up my profile on datemedotcom? It was true that anyone growing up in Ireland would have at least a rudimentary understanding of Gaelic but how the fuck did he know that? I had always been terrible at Gaelic. I never managed to get even a pass on all the test papers I'd taken and now because I couldn't think of the response to this basic question I was going to be incarcerated in Canada.

And then slowly from somewhere uninvited, maybe because my internal editors were not yet at their desks, a deep sense of dread began to overtake me like a huge abstract ink-stain widening within me. Would I be strip-searched by this gargantuan? Each of his fingers was bigger than my dick. He reached into a drawer where I suspected he kept his rubber gloves. I was about to lose my virginity to a Mountie.

He took out a stapler.

When I was finally allowed to make a call I was so happy to hear our receptionist mispronounce the initials of the agency, (so many egos jostling for attention) I almost cried. She put me through to our legal guy and suddenly it was as if the Lord God Himself spake unto me.

"We've had this happen before. You can help Silvestro and Lucien in our European office while we figure this out."

It certainly seemed like a reasonable solution but I was surprised he was able to suggest it with such confidence. My Irish passport allowed me to work anywhere in Europe but did the agency lawyer have the power to just send me there? Surely such an idea would need to be run past Andy. Not if he already knew about it.

Either way, I had just agreed to be sent to the most precarious place on the planet for a recovering alcoholic and budding sex-addict. Or the most convenient depending on your point of view.

2

Hi there, I'm a newly arrived writer from New York, and I'm sitting out here on the balcony of my Prinsengracht office looking out on the canal. As I type this, I'm having to half-close my laptop because there's a squirrel (or at least I hope it's a squirrel) above me munching on something left out by my upstairs neighbour and as a result there is some serious crumb-spillage onto my keyboard... so if I stat to moss up my werds as I tip I'm hape you'll firgove me??? But what has all this got to do with you?? Well I don't want you to feel bad but I'm supposed to be working on my second book, the Notoriously Difficult Second Book (hey, that might be a good title) but after seeing your beautiful picture my concentration went out the window. You could say I'm out here trying to find it. Write soon or I won't be able to.

The profiles in the Amsterdam section of

datemedotcom were mostly made up of East European immigrants and British expats working for international companies lured there by generous tax concessions. And judging from the repeated references to books, films and music by the likes of William Burroughs, Lars Von Trier and Leonard Cohen it was obvious to even the untrained eye that a morbid intelligence prevailed. Unlike their American counterparts who took great pains to appear content and companionable at all times, the attitude here was openly suicidal.

Maybe it was all that rain.

I had hoped that my happy-go-lucky imperson- ation of a newly arrived writer might go some way towards alleviating the mood but my empty inbox seemed to indicate that I would have to do better than squirrels if I was going to get laid in Amsterdam. And yes, the red-light district was minutes away but paying for sex was unacceptable. It took all the charm out of it. If anything, it was *too* honest.

Earlier on that Sunday afternoon, before letting myself into our elegant Prinsengracht offices, I attended an English-speaking AA meeting on the Oude ZijdsVorrburwal (good luck pronouncing it) and after a brief conversation with a local man called Erik I was able to glean that online dating wasn't nearly as accepted in Amsterdam as I had hoped. In fact when Erik finally managed to absorb the idea into his comprehension his nose twitched involuntarily like he had just smelled something awful in the air around us.

This from an alcoholic-ex-junkie-wife-beater.

Online dating didn't just reek of desperation. It

was worse than that. It smacked of America. Meanwhile these immigrant girls were unfucked and far from home in a country where it rained hourly and fits of coughing stood in for conversation. Of course they were miserable.

From downstairs, the sounds of pedestrians out on the Prinsengracht mingled for a moment with the muttering of two men's voices before the front door closed again. Next came an insistent pounding which I quickly learned was the result of two people ascending the stairs. Lucien, with his black lifeless eyes scanning the floor ahead of him, was first to enter the room and he continued apparently unaware of my presence, to his desk. Equally intense and similarly preoccupied, he was followed by Silvestro Da Gemi, the black-bearded creative director of the Amsterdam office.

I began to hope that what I was witnessing was the silence that follows a heated argument since any difficulty in their relationship might be an opportunity for me, but watching them settle in at adjacent desks without so much as a nod of recognition to me I realised I couldn't have been more wrong. In fact, the velocity of their agreement would soon become apparent in the form of an award-winning ad campaign called The Life Less Driven.

I coughed and shuffled in my seat and when neither of them looked up I had to assume I was being ignored and that my presence was indeed an inconvenience. It was true I had been sent there by their so-called superiors but they were obviously above all that. This was Amsterdam. Lucien was a Parisian, Silvestro was a Roman and I was just some guy who had fucked up his travel arrangements. In fact I was a homeless person.

Mortified by datemedotcom's pink glow, I began to understand why Frida, our HR lady, had been so reluctant to give me the alarm code for the building that previous Friday. I thought it was because nobody worked on the weekends in laid-back Amsterdam but it was obvious now she knew Silvestro and Lucien were coming in and would not welcome distractions. I couldn't tell her I only wanted to check out the local pussy and she couldn't tell me they didn't want me working on the new campaign.

But I *was* there and even though I wished I could disappear I couldn't. I knew what they were working on because I had been cc'd on the brief. It was the same brief as always Make Safety Interesting. I was expected to work on it with them but I knew they'd kill any idea of mine before I even uttered it. And yet if I was to justify being taken into their fold I'd need to at least pretend to come up with something. I stared at my screen. Now I was miserable too.

Norwegian summers are short and the resident reindeer needs to make the most of the newly sprouted pastures. The more he fattens in preparation for the cold months ahead the more attractive he becomes to the other local resident, the mosquito. Before long, the huge antklered animal is barely visible through a whining hovering haze; not so much a reindeer being harassed by mosquitoes but a cloud of mosquitoes in the shape of a reindeer. The humidity combined with the moisture from the fiords provides the ideal breeding ground for the mosquito. And for the reindeer-herders, a swarm of mosquitoes is better than a sheep-dog. They wait chatting and smoking on higher cooler ground for the exhausted beasts to shuffle meekly into harness. But this one, not content with being bullied uphill kicks and bucks as he tries to unseat the multitude. He escapes into sharp focus only to succumb once more to the blur. This is repeated until the energy expended requires a return to grazing which is apparently unacceptable because suddenly the reindeer-shaped mosquito-cloud ejects a real-life reindeer into one fresh, clean, breezy moment of freedom and the Fiord below.

YORTA

"I love your reindeer story. I definitely identify."

In all of Deadkween's very black and very white profile pictures she appeared luminously beautiful in sultry poses wearing an assortment of black leather and lingerie. In one particularly successful picture she paid homage to Charlotte Rampling's famous pose from Night Porter complete with long sleeved evening-gloves and Nazi hat. She was lost-looking in a soon-to-be dead-sort-of-way. As if her last earthy exhalation would be in orgasm. She owned a small gallery in Berlin called Poisoned Resevoir and visited Amsterdam regularly "for inspiration." She wrote poems and attached them to her hand-made dead-baby-dolls. I was allowed to know this much over the phone but she waited until we met to tell me she was an Albino who dyed her hair black and wore contact lenses. I never met an actual albino before.

She certainly was very pale but no more than I'd

seen on a Dublin bus. It immediately explained why all her pictures were black and white and why she looked so good in them. We were on her black leather couch at this point in her black-walled apartment overlooking the Vondelpark and though it was still early it was almost totally dark in there. The drawn blinds and veils draped over the lights didn't help. She could only be exposed to daylight for a limited length of time each day. All signs indicated that I was about to fuck my first Vampire until I declined a beer in favor of a water.

"You're not in AA are you?"

"Well, actually yes. I am."

I left a gap for the inevitable gush of admiration.

"I. Fucking. Hate. AA."

It turned out that her alcoholic-heroin-addict-ex-husband had been in AA for a while and his sponsor insisted that she attend meetings too. But while she sat in Alanon meetings her hubby sold the furniture. When she confronted him about it he threw her down the same stairs we'd just ascended. She pointed almost proudly to the areas of her face where she'd had surgery. The rhinoplasty had cost extra. If she ever tracked him down she would round up some of the boys and have the word Rapist tattooed on his forehead. It was at this point that she mentioned that her best friend was President of The Hell's Angels in Amsterdam. I could have used that water now but I was too afraid to speak. Still recovering from the shock of uncovering an AA member in her own home, she now sought reassurance.

"But you do have the job?" I nodded carefully.

"And the apartment?"

The Job? The Apartment? Like two out of three wasn't bad. Like I had lied about everything else. She continued as if none of what she had just said could possibly have any effect on what she was about to say. What she wanted, she said, was to settle down and have a child. She was ready. Was I ready?

Somewhat calmed now that she was talking about her future she sank back into the couch revealing a tattooed white star only barely visible against the white skin of her midriff. It was a Pentagram.

Of course it was.

She would obviously be demonic in bed but a good fuck was a small reward for what she really wanted. Luminous babies and eternal darkness.

Suddenly my natural paranoia, which until then had been gathering facts in a half-awake, half-interested manner awoke with a jolt. She was obviously pregnant and the plan was to first fuck me and then dupe me into bringing up the her pasty progeny as my own.What was happening here? Was it the suicidal reindeer? I looked down at my feet to find that I was descending the stairs with only slightly more dignity than she had when she'd been thrown down them.

*****

"I never got to thank you for all the work. It's going well isn't it?"

Johnathan, our very British account manager, appeared genuine enough but an account man's work was never done. He might need me to work late, or let him kill an idea he couldn't sell or come in to work on a weekend. This was his way of sounding me out. So, when I redirected his gratitude to Silvestro, his eyes narrowed. A creative who didn't gloam at easy praise was something to be wary of. Did I know something he didn't? Was this campaign about to be received less favourably than he'd been led to believe? Why would I deflect the credit for a potentially award-winning campaign?

The preliminary research results indicated that The Life Less Driven was a winner. It had already tested through the roof in London, Berlin, Los Angeles and New York. The idea was simple. Demonstrate safety by showing the driver and passenger conversing freely. Real conversations. The more relaxed the conversation, the safer the car. The client loved it because the car was in every single shot and creatives aspired to it because the conversations were real. It went beyond advertising. It was reality with a logo.

Christoph, our German producer had referred to it, in an all-staff email as the Irishman's campaign. This was something he would only do if Silvestro had already sanctioned it. My first impulse was to send out a reply-to-all saying I'd had nothing to do with it. But if the creative director wanted it said that I was involved in this campaign then who was I to object? Maybe it was his generous gesture of welcome? His way of including me. I also had to tread carefully since my visa-situation had become extremely delicate. The lawyer was now saying my "little hiccup" at the Canadian border could effectively halt my green card application and because of this here was a very real danger I might never work in the US again. This was not the time to distance myself from an award winning campaign. And anyway hadn't I perpetrated enough good work of my own over the years to piggy-back just this once?

Across the room, Lucien sat straight-backed and expressionless watching me carefully as if he might draw me later from memory. Without taking those button-black eyes from mine his fingers began typing so fast I thought at first he was joking. The screen in front of him was as indecipherable as he was. Macro enlargements of half-tone photography woven into layers of transparent type, ground up against jagged slabs of flat black and white. All strangely haphazard and definately non-commercial. It was like an aerial view of some unforgiving alien landscape, impenetrably obscure, airless and unwelcoming. It was obvious from even a distance that it wasn't agency work. It soon became clear from the galleys and layouts strewn over every available surface of the three-story canal house that Lucien's book of black and white photography (mostly black) would soon be published thanks to agency funds set aside by Silvestro. It would be his reward for past services and, as far as I could see it was the only reason he tolerated any of us at all.

What I didn't know was that he had already resigned. As soon as his books were delivered he would be gone. Was it just co-incidence that I should end up in Amsterdam just as he was leaving? It might have been paranoia but a scenario began to emerge that seemed to explain everything. Maybe Andy had intentionally orchestrated the shoot in Canada knowing that my visa was up for renewal. He wasn't exactly pleased when he caught me printing out my book and even less so when I made that comment in the toilet. And with Lucien leaving they needed someone to help Silvestro. Andy could get rid of me and find a use for me at the same time. It made sense. As creative director it would have been easy to find out the status of my work visa. If this was true then I might have to accept that Amsterdam was now my permanent home.

PIPPA
Pippa was an upper-class British girl whose idea of slumming it was to fuck someone like me. She was fat little fucker but her accent seemed to suggest otherwise. As if body fat was something only the lower classes suffered from. Daddy, a politician in the Hague would no doubt be suitably livid when she inferred between Dover Sole and Gooseberry Fool that she'd bedded a Mick. I probably made as much money if not more than he did but I wanted her to see me as a bohemian writer mostly because I wanted to believe it myself.

She drove a tiny MG sports car that she constantly felt the need to apologise for. She said in a faraway voice that I looked like a Labrador and I somehow knew by this that we were going to have sex.

When she took her clothes off she expanded like dough and at one point I inserted myself into what I hoped was her pussy but there was a very real fear that it might be a sweaty fold in her lower bellies. I tried to give the impression I was enjoying the sensation so much I had to close my eyes but she wasn't having it.

"Open your eyes, would you?"

The teenage models I had conjured in my mind exploded as I suddenly became a sexual plate-spinner trying to keep her nipples erect so that at least I could tell what was tit and what was not. When she got on top of me I had to suppress an urge to fight. I was beginning to doubt if I could actually orgasm under all that heaving girl-flesh, until she had the decency to reach down and insert one of her fat fingers in my butthole.

I ejaculated immediately.

Flushed with relief, I turned to her, grateful that I'd never have to see her again.

"I felt something in there," she whispered," you might want to have it looked at."

My hard-won swirl of endorphins soured inside me.

*****

"Apple-sick duck the fuck?"

The receptionist thought I was Dutch.

"I have an appointment with Dr. Van Rossem." I explained.

"I'll tell him you're here"

It would seem silly later, childish even, but the thought that I would die from stress-induced cancer of the colon had for the two preceding weeks occupied the width and breath of my being. Advertising had killed me. Pippa's post-coital concern merely confirmed what I had already feared. I'd die elegantly in nearby France while my medical insurance was still eligible. At least I wouldn't have to be insulted by spoken Dutch ever again. But my almost comforting death-wish was short-lived when, after administering a gentle lunchtime probing to my virgin sphincter, the doctor declared me benign. I felt relief and then joy. And then relief again. It occurred to me that I had been at least as frightened of getting an erection as a bad diagnosis. You could say I got the all-clear in more than one sense. Mind you, he was an ugly fucker.

This commercial opens with an over-the-shoul-der-shot of me writing on my laptop. The camera zooms in on the screen until we are looking at what appears to be an extreme close-up of two equal sized dots positioned one on top of the other. It's a colon.

•

•

We hear a woman's soothing voice say; "*Getting checked early can seriously increase your chances of survival.*" Dissolve as the camera settles into the next close-up. One dot positioned over a comma, a semi-colon.

•

,

"*Getting checked when the disease has already set in can prove more difficult to treat.*" The next frame shows only one solitary dot. A period.

•

"*Get checked early for colon cancer before it's too late.*" Issued by Center For Cancer Research

----

VALERIYA

With Silvestro, Christoph and Johnathan away in Reykjavik shooting the first instalment of The Life Less Driven, I was left to look after the agency. Four more shoots would follow in Hong Kong, Berlin, Lisbon, and Rome. Silvestro had invited me to take his place but it was wrapped in an unspoken expectation that I should stay. It was pure diplomacy. Olaffson had just signed off on a pan-European campaign that had no script and they weren't about to have it supervised by a guy who couldn't even remember to bring proper travel documents on his last shoot. I knew this and Silvestro knew this. But it needed to look like my decision because this was supposedly my campaign.

And anyway I had far more important matters on my mind. Namely, a third date with the beautiful Valeriya. After a giggly visit to the Reich Museum (me popping out from behind the exhibits like a child surprising his mother) she opened her lovely mouth and changed everything. In the café down-stairs she described her many trips to Florence while sympathising with me for never having been. She said I couldn't call myself a real writer until I visited Florence at least once. She went on to say that she would have gone there even more often if the choice had been hers to make but that was what life was like when you're...

This was where I experienced what Hitchcock liked to call a reverse-smile. When he couldn't trust an actor's skills he relied instead on certain tricks like beginning a shot with an existing smile and then asking for it to be removed. This gave him the option of playing the sequence in reverse. It was also a subtle insult to the actors who were understandably upset by this practice and no doubt performed the perfect reverse-smile when they were introduced to the idea. He would have loved the effect on my face when I heard the word *married*. I felt sick and tricked because I realised I had been effortlessly manipulated into wanting her more than I actually did.

The options were Single, Separated or Divorced. She had selected Single. She suddenly seemed second-hand. Used even. Of course you're married my expression tried to say. Isn't everyone? I tried to effect nonchalance. It would buy me some time to think. Maybe this kind of behaviour was standard online. And maybe, just maybe, my instinctual knee-jerk response of you fucking lying cunt didn't apply. At least not yet. Then it occurred to me that if she had lied to me it meant I didn't need to be so respect-ful any more. I'd already spent hours daydreaming about us making love but now I just wanted to fuck her. And soon, before I found out something else I didn't want to hear. I suggested we drop by my place for desert and when she agreed I thought even less of her.

There was a pause in my doorway as if there was a chance she might not go in but I took this to be just another lie, her playing the part of a timid girl so I could feel more powerful. So be it. I pushed the door open and before she crossed the threshold I had peeled her coat and blouse away in one. Her nipples seemed strangely sunken like those of an older woman but otherwise she was a like a fucking movie star.

"You're like a fucking movie star." I said.

Her long slim girlish legs shivered apart at my touch and I licked her out and she gave me a sloppy slippery blow-job. She'd been very sneaky about not telling me she was married. In fact she was still married. We were committing adultery. Or at least she was. I wanted to ask if she had really been a figure skater or was that a lie too? I couldn't be sure what was true and what wasn't. To confuse matters even more the sex was beautiful and loving and dirty all at the same time. She was married. So what? As she teased the tip of my cock with the tip of her tongue I didn't care if she turned out to be a man. She had a great energy and was cheerful and full of life and laughter and her pussy was the most beautiful I had ever seen in real life. It was so perfectly symmetrical I dubbed it pussuq.

She stretched her foot down to stroke my dick as I lapped at her. Was this a trick she used on her husband? Of course it was. I could have stayed down there all day. There was never any need to explain anything to Valeriya she intuitively under-stood. At one point I sat with my pants around my knees, half crouched to absorb the shocks as she smashed her pussuq down onto my cock like she was trying to kill something. as she began to exhaust herself on my midriff I gathered her to me and waddled ankle-panted across the floor to lay her down there so I could more easily feast on her. But I wasn't allowed. Springing back up on her bare feet she bid me kneel and immediately began pummelling me mercilessly with spat-on hands like some sexual laborer.

"Come on, give it to me." It was as if I was withholding her property. Until then it had seemed too rude to unload the contents of my loins at a girl l but from the look on this girl's face it began to look like it might be insulting not to. Three white arcs loosed themselves into the void between us. The first two disappeared out of view but the last clung like a smile to her heaving breasts. I bayed like a dog at an imaginary moon and we hugged for so long after coming I felt like we'd been stirred together like milk in tea. No sugar. And because she was unavailable it was ok to fall in love with her.

"Come on now, be honest, wouldn't you be a slut if you were a girl?"

The question didn't seem fair because everyone knew girls just didn't think like that. But here was a girl, a beautiful girl asking me a question that demanded the reorganisation of everything I'd ever thought about women. I was suddenly seized with a desire not so much to have her but to be her. I was jealous of her freedom. Her power. A great looking girl could fuck anyone she wanted. Surely such power was intoxicating. She was like a guy in a girl's body. Girls weren't supposed to think like this. Maybe all girls thought like this and Valeriya was just willing to admit it. She accused me of analysing everything and pronounced it *anal-ising*. I couldn't tell if this was because English was her second language and therefore a coincidence or whether she had effortlessly out-punned me.

"If you were a girl wouldn't you be a slut?" she repeated the question as if it was a natural progression from what she had just said and in the full knowledge that I was defeated I conceded reluctantly, that yes, I would.

"Well there you go."

She said it like it explained everything but all it did was confuse me even more. She saw herself as a slut? She knew how to adapt to whatever conditions presented her. It was classic behaviour of abused children. We learn how to keep the peace at the expense of our own needs. We merge into any given situation. When two chameleons successfully take on each other's hues there is nothing there. Supplying her with a list of film contacts was laughably easy for me but I resisted until the last moment in the vain hope that she might say she didn't want them. That she loved me. That I was what she wanted. I knew that as soon as I sent that email it would conclude our business. Her response said it all.

"I don't know how to thank you. Well I do, but let's pretend."

Especially the last two words.

ANICA

Anica was a long-necked Slovakian systems analyst for a pharmaceutical company based in the Hague. In the time I knew her she visibly brightened only twice. Once when she swallowed an entire glass of whiskey in one gulp, and once when she talked about her combat-training as a child.

"I am proficient with a Kalashnikof."

I had hopes for some heavy petting and a handful of arse in preparation for a full-on-fuck which I wanted to suggest would be the following Saturday. When she turned up that first night there was a very tall good-looking guy close behind her so I assumed they were a couple and I was already eyeing her up when she broke away from him and stood there in front of me. I didn't stand up in case I only came up to her shoulder. She was tall, but surmountable. I told myself that her expression indicated satisfaction with what she saw too. This was always a tricky moment. Great care had to be taken not to let your true feelings of nervousness or disappointment creep into your face. We had no knowledge of each other's facial eccentricities. Two complete strangers willingly engaged in an artificially arranged attempt at falling in love. If we allowed dissatisfaction into our faces we immediately made ourselves uglier thereby setting off a reaction in the other person's face that limited the chances of either of us looking our best which in turn only increased the possibility of repulsion.

Hence our crazy smiles.

Her linen trousers were virtually transparent and her tits were pert and she seemed to be at right angles to herself. All in all, very Slavic. She drank two glasses of wine at dinner and a Jameson's at the bar afterwards. She asked me what whiskey I would recommend as an alcoholic so I ordered the Jameson's for her. More than once she started to reach for it and stopped herself. It was the sort of jesture that uninterrupted would have resulted in her gulping the entire glass down thereby requiring another to be ordered. I recognised this muffled yearning only too well. The injustice of having a whiskey in front of you, when it should be inside you. Anything Dutch bored her. We had that much in common. By then I was looking at her the same way she was looking at her glass. She hated Holland but couldn't leave. She said her friends considered her a pain in the ass after she'd had a few drinks.

"In that case you can count me among your friends" I said.

She smiled and tilted her head as if I had just paid her a compliment.

"You should take your hand away from you mouth when you talk, it makes you look dishonest." she said.

I could see how she could be a real bitch. But I wouldn't let her. She certainly liked her booze. Three glasses of wine that first night.

"Do you have many friends that drink?"

I put my hand in front of my mouth.

"Yes" I said.

She laughed at this, reluctantly.

The next night we met she wasn't drinking because she was afraid of making me uncomfortable which had the effect of making her uncomfortable instead. In fact she became frighteningly depressing. Had she necked a couple of whiskeys I would have been the one exhaling in relief. The result was that she didn't look so good to me and in her cowboy boots she appeared even taller. We cowered in some god-awful seaside restaurant that looked like it might have been on the shores of the Styx as angry white-knuckled waves tried repeatedly to grip the mainland and drag it under.

I tried manfully to keep things light.

"So how was your day?"

"I'm not in a cheerful mood."

"Oh I'm sorry to hear that. Bad day at work?"

"I just heard that my friend has cancer."

I was sorry to hear that too because now I was

going to have to listen to this shit all night. Cancer; the alcoholic's friend. Nobody could laugh when cancer was in the room. It must have been killing her. She was looking for an excuse to drink and she even had a good one but I was sitting there in front of her the sober alcoholic.

At the end of the evening I tried to kiss her more from duty than desire but she almost snapped her neck pulling away. It would have been more depressing if I hadn't even tried. Was there such a thing as a nice pretty girl who wasn't divorced, married or crazy? Was that possible? Anica, on closer inspection was a communist-built structure teetering on the brink of collapse. I still wanted to at least see her naked.

"Wow."

"Wow? What does this mean? Wow?"

"The passion." I said.

"I'm deciding if I should go or stay."

"And you're short." she added. It was with a smile but she said it.

"It doesn't matter when you're lying down."

"You're not lying down all the time."

I wanted to tell her to go fuck herself but after coming all the way to the Hague I felt I was owed something. Something I could still get if I was patient.

"You could be a sweet guy but you hide behind the jokes."she said at last.

Then she told me she was married and I hardly even heard her. When Valeriya told me the same thing I nearly broke in half. She lived with her husband of seven years in a very respectable neighbourhood in Haarlem. I was suddenly thinking about Valeriya I couldn't unerstand how she'd become so deeply embedded in my being. Like an arrow that hurt less if it was allowed to remain in place. Anica was almost waving now as she tried to get my attention. She invited me back to a depressingly large mostly white apartment. Didn't she say she had a husband somewhere? Was this where she took her online dates? Would the husband walk in any second? The moment we got inside she turned around and kissed me. I had no idea she would be so feminine and gentle under all that Slavic frost. We shed our clothes like they'd just turned poisonous. With her hair down around those slender shoulders she was a different person. Sweet even. She whispered to me as I fucked her.

"I love it, yessss, oh baby, yes ohhhhh nice, yes, nail me."

Nail me?

She got on top and let her hair fall over me like darkness and I laughed out loud when she orgasmed because the sounds she made were so feminine and innocent and so gratifying to the ears of someone as jaded as me, I assumed she was faking. But then I saw the tell-tale red patches on her neck and chest as if her body was blushing. And as her taut stomach shivered against mine with my cock still hard inside there I began to feel something other than just lust for her. It was gratitude. The sort of gratitude you feel when someone who has done you a great kindness. There was a selflessness about her in that moment that was endearing. I had never made a girl come like that before. And the fact that I hadn't come yet merely confirmed my status as stud.

I'd give her a rest before going again.

And so lying there beneath her limp perspiring body with her knees either side of me and her hair spilled across my face, I began to talk about Valeriya. How she had lied to me. How I was better off without her. How she saw herself as a slut. I couldn't stop myself. I even mentioned the lure of the pussuq. Anica made encouraging sounds. She was hearing my confession, making me truly hers. Minutes passed before I realised she was snoring. She had fucked me and fallen asleep.

REBECCA

Rebecca's profile picture showed her straining against the confines of a skin-tight mini-dress in mid-Tango. The faceless silhouetted male with whom she danced was obviously for presentation purposes only. Look at my scorching hot body. This was how she wanted to be seen on a dating site. In her other picture, a close-up, she looked like the aging mother of the girl on the dance-floor.

Following her father's nervous breakdown Rebecca was sent to live with his brother (her uncle) and aunt in Germany. He would be her first sexual experience when he made her come with his fingers. She was fifteen.

"So he abused you?'

"Yes I suppose so, but he didn't go all the way." I was reminded of how I had defended Brother Ollie, because in defending him I could convince myself I had actually wanted my balls fondled by a clergy-man. It was sad to think of all that sexuality locked up inside the conservative life of an English teacher in Amsterdam. She looked like she was holding her breath permanently. But after one kiss Agatha

Christie became Julie Christie and yes she had the accent to match. You need six hundred years of British oppression stored away in your DNA to appreciate the satisfaction of thrusting your undeserving Irish cock into a mouth that has just finished saying; "Darling, I've been frightfully busy today."

Fucking her took on political status.

"This is for. The Famine and this is for. Bloody. Sunday. This is for. Maggie Thatcher and this? This is for Princess Dianaaaaaagggggh."

On rain-soaked Mondays, which in the Netherlands are indistinguishable from every other day, she cheered herself up by appearing in front of her class wearing a light grey one-piece boiler suit that showed off her lithe body to full effect. When she turned to write on the chalkboard the class fell silent. For most teachers it was the other way round. It was an honor, she said, to be part of their sexual awakening. She intentionally made spelling mistakes knowing full well that she would first need to bend and reach for the eraser before shaking herself vigorously as she scrubbed it away. She delighted in the idea of these boys pummelling themselves at home under the blankets with the image of her superb ass coaxing them out of puberty.

And she loved to suck me off. It was the first thing she'd do. I began to suspect that her uncle had taught her well. The moment before she reached orgasm she would look at me like she'd just been grossly insulted. As if in the middle of fucking her I'd said; "Rebecca, you are a sad-faced English bitch who I'm only fucking as a favor." She looked at that moment like she was being overtaken not by ecstasy but a shuddering exhalation of abhorrence. As if all the platitudes and denials burned away and there beyond the mists and veils for just one instant before being engulfed again was the truth; she was fucking a Mick.

OLGA
"You live a charmed life."
Seeing myself through the jealous eyes of my house-guest felt unexpectedly good. Josh was only half way through his first day and he'd already visited the red light district and two of its prostitutes before we even got back to my place.

Josh was a sexual tourist and I was his base.

I'd gotten to know him just enough in St LaCroix to invite him to visit me in New York but he never took me up on it because I suppose New York didn't offer the same sexual possibilities as Amsterdam. And more recently he had fallen in love with a Russian girl and so a few days layover in Amsterdam seemed to him to be a good idea before continuing on to Moscow. It transpired after only a little questioning that the girl in Moscow whom he talked about marrying was in fact a self-confessed... I didn't dare say the word in front of him because he was convinced she was in love with him too.

Josh was what I imagined every hooker dreamt of. A constant source of employment. He talked a lot about asking her to come and live with him in Saint La Croix. In the meantime had selected a rather buxom girl who wouldn't have been my first choice but it was his money not mine. While I wait-
e   d

outside for him I noticed a girl in a window to the right who, when she thought no-one was looking took swigs from a tall glistening black bottle and surreptitiously stroked the white tail of a cat hidden behind her little bed. The tail straightened between her slender fingers like some headless python or yes I suppose, a penis. I had already spent more time than was healthy waiting on the little brown bricked bridge as Josh fucked the girl-next-door. Defiling such a wholesome phrase would have appealed to him. I began to see how this worked. These scarlet windows were no different from the covers of fashion magazines in the more respectable bookstores across town from which similar girls simpered. One informed the other.

And it wasn't just men who got off on it. Women sauntered past smiling knowingly as if they recognised something familiar about it all. Maybe they were reassured by the fact that if you were alluring enough or just there enough (some of the prostitutes were unmentionably ugly) you too would eventually attract your man. Here, sexual attraction was reduced to its barest necessities. There was no literature here, no Elizabethan poems just naked sexual honesty. The yearning of bodily organs for each other. It was so practical. So very Dutch. You want sex. We have it.

Josh finally emerged without even a trace of a smile. He preferred them not to make any oooh and ahhh sounds.

"I appreciate it if they just stay quiet. I always tell them this in advance. If they charge one-fifty I'll put three hundred down so I have some room for maneuver."

I was impressed by this no-nonsense approach but it was a paradoxical to me. I would need to believe they wanted me. Wasn't this what was on sale? The illusion that a young beautiful woman was aroused by me? But maybe he was right. By letting them know he wasn't interested in their performance he retained control of the situation. And control was the real commodity here. The need to decide if they meant it was removed. He already knew they didn't mean it so why should he have to suffer their bad acting? He said he couldn't come with the buxom hooker because she spoke to him and in doing so she broke the sexual equivalent of the fourth wall.

"Have you been smokink maruijana?" he mimicked her "you only get ze one position." and when he couldn't come; "Maybe you should cut it off, ja?"

He picked up his bag with the airport tags still attached and we were about to head back to my place when he noticed the girl with the Liebfraumilch beckoning and even though she gyrated amateurish and giggled unconvincingly I felt a stirring. Josh didn't know that she was beckoning at me. He didn't know and he didn't care. I tried to find some way to claim her as my own. I'd seen her first. Surely he wasn't about to just go and fuck her so soon after the last one? She was a prostitute and as such she was doing what a prostitutes do. She was standing there nearly naked in a window offering sex for money with full governmental approval.

And yes of course I wanted her but I couldn't bring myself to visit a prostitute because it meant I'd have to confront the idea that all sexual attraction was based on a transaction. That men wanted sex and women wanted security. My ego just couldn't handle the notion that any male would do. She had winked at me while I waited for Josh and now she was going to fuck him? Josh dropped his bag again and looked at me. He could see something was going on.

"I won't be long." he said.

The uninvited heat of jealousy invaded my thoughts and my initial almost naïve sexual fervour for the girl in the window dissolved into disgust first for her and then hatred for the entire female gender who it seemed waved their pussies in front of us, to get a washing machine, a raise, a new dress or a free dinner. When he came out I searched his face for some sign of pleasure or relief or shame or mischievousness.

"I fucked her in the ass." he said.

It disgusted me to think that by being there I had inadvertently added to his pleasure. I was as jealous and enraged as if he had fucked my girlfriend. I felt wronged but what could I say? There was no conceivable way to justify what I was feeling. I was jealous that Josh had fucked a prostitute. I called my sponsor and he suggested I tell Josh to get a hotel room and this exactly what I did. Josh wasn't even surprised when I told him I disagreed with what he was doing and that I felt it was not sober behaviour. It was as if he wanted me to throw him out so that he could think even less of himself than he already did.

This commercial opens on a shot of me in Albert Hein Supermarket. I take out my credit card and swipe it in the self-service consul. A green light flickers and we hear an automated voice. "Alstublieft." (In subtitles we see that this means *thank you*) Lowering the groceries into a cart I wheel them away. Cut to another scenario. This time I'm buying some new clothes and swiping my credit card as the same greeting appears in friendly flashing typeface. "Alstublieft" I exit the store with my shopping bags. Cut to an interior of my apartment. I'm wearing the clothes I bought earlier and with the groceries I've prepared a beautiful dinner for two. The doorbell sounds and after one last look at the table to make sure everything is in place I open the door to reveal a stunningly beautiful girl standing in the doorway. But before she enters the apartment she holds out her hand for my credit card. Taking it from me she reaches up under her skirt and she appears to insert the card between her legs. She smiles politely as if waiting for the results to come through before her eyes widen and a huge seductive smile spreads across her face. She hands the card back to me.

"Alstublieft." she says seductively and steps into the apartment. A title appears on the screen; "God is Good But Business Is Better" Issued by the The Dutch Institute of Commerce.

PAMELA
"Tell me he's going with you, you can't not bring him."

In taking up my cause like this, Pamela, my newly employed assistant, made it appear like

Johnathan wasn't about to invite me to the awards ceremony when for all any of us knew he might have come upstairs to do exactly that. Such a strategy would make her popular with me, because she was fighting my corner, and get rid of me at the same time. She was hired when Lucien left because I had none of his computer skills. She was fluent in Photoshop, Indesign, After Effects and many other programmes I hadn't even heard of. Also recommending her for the job was the fact there was no danger of anything even vaguely sexual ever transpiring between us since she had difficulty squeezing herself in, and extricating herself from, between the armrests of a normal-sized chair. (Mind you, it hadn't stopped me before). This seemed to suggest that my superiors knew more about my proclivities than I realised.

In any case, her substantial presence made mine even less relevant. She could easily make all the adaptations necessary for the print ads and posters, which was all that was left to do now that The Life Less Driven was running across Europe. In fact there was now no need at all for me to be in Amsterdam apart from the fact that I had been deported. This was the term being used in agency emails to describe my situation. But Pamela was no mere technician she was also the self-appointed curator of the Agency Celebrity Phone List.

Hilarious, if like Silvestro, you resembled the classic Italian film star Mario Mercelli, or like Christoph, you were often mistaken for the Dutch footballer Erik Van Beek. But what if you looked like Uncle Fester? The Agency Celebrity Phone list sat laminated on every desk by every phone so that every photographer, illustrator, visiting client or pizza-delivery-guy saw your name and extension under an image of Uncle Fester. And what was worse, no one was confused by it.

Was this Pamela's revenge for making her work so late and so often while I rummaged around online looking for women? Seeing the trauma in my face the first day it appeared and perhaps fearing retribution in the form of even more late night sessions duplicating even more layouts, she confessed.

"Silvestro said to find a picture of Uncle Fester. I didn't know what it was for."

I thought she got off light as the Shrek's wife. But Johnathan (Colin Firth), just smiled graciously and handed me a large manila envelope full of mail diverted from the New York office. I knew without opening it that it contained director's showreels and photographer's brochures beseeching me for work. It was probably the only reason he had stopped by but now that Pamela had shamed him into it, he did indeed invite me and I of course accepted because what kind of a crazy bastard would refuse an all expenses paid trip to the Cannes Advertising Awards?

They only gave Titanium Awards when something was so fabulously wonderful they felt it needed a special category all to itself. The Life Less Driven fell under just such a category. I wanted to call someone and share the news but there was no one. I thought of Rebecca but what was the point? She'd be moving to Berlin in a few weeks and she'd have a new man within the month. My mother wouldn't even understand and even if she did all she'd want to hear was whether there was some money in it for her. My sponsor? He'd feel obliged to congratulate me but so what?

"Congratulations, and don't forget to share your gratitude at a meeting… oh and don't drink."

The ceremony wasn't until 8pm so we could have easily flown in later in the day but because Johnathan wanted to get away from his horrific wife I had to get up at 6am on a Saturday morning to meet the flight he'd booked for us. He could see I wasn't very happy about it.

"You'll thank me later when we have a nice dinner."

He smelled to me like he was still drunk from the night before. I couldn't summon even token excitement at the prospect of receiving the equivalent of an Oscar for a campaign I'd had nothing to do with.

We hadn't even taken off yet and I couldn't wait to get back. By the time we were ushered onto the stage that night after an eternity of delayed flights and a torturously slow cab ride from the airport I felt like I'd been out-maneuvered yet again. I'd only just managed to get into my shitty little hotel room when I Johnathan called to say we were already late. I only just had time to change before jumping in a cab.

Onstage Silvestro, Christoph and Johnathan wore simple white shirts and comfortable jeans. Had they agreed on what to wear? They effortlessly exuded the demeanour of talented people accustomed to the logistics or receiving awards. Their light-colored clothes deflected the heat of the spotlights while I stood there in my black cowboy shirt, black jeans and crepe-soled brothel creepers, staring at them in consternation. I looked like the guy who had no connection with the other three. I had become the American who didn't get it. Between camera-flashes I remember looking out at the rows of faces each of them seemingly searching for something up on the stage. What did they see? The area around my feet was scratched and scuffed and over-lit and just seemed dirty. There was dandruff on the photographer and feedback from the microphones. The curtain was frayed and the music was canned, the applause reluctant, the podium perspex. This was the view from the top?

MARIEKE

Later, Silvestro, Christoph and Johnathan held court in the Noisette D'or, and sitting next to Silvestro was a girl so beautiful she all but rendered him invisible. She was so insultingly beautiful I felt an inexplicable urge to retaliate at someone or some-thing. I was invited to sit down and watch them all get drunk.

"Hi, I'm Marieke, I don't think we've met?"

Marieke, I decided, had developed an expression of perpetual severity so that mortal man might be spared the full brunt of her allure. So flattering was her beauty in its relaxed state that even the weakest smile ignited fantasies. When she told the table she and her boyfriend had bought a place in Amsterdam and then split up, every face brightened involuntari-ly and then checked themselves. She was after all, Silvestro's property now. Johnathan seemed to have developed a maddening itch on his upper arm that required him to push back the sleeve of a t-shirt that ordinarily concealed his Maori-style tattoo from clients. Christoph, already quite drunk, continuously took pictures of himself and whoever else was near so that presumably the following morning he could consult the digital oracle for clues as to what had happened the night before. His camera turned blackouts into brownouts. There was an ad for cameras in there somewhere. Meanwhile Silvestro was trying very hard not to get caught ogling the up-turned braless breasts of his unbearably beautiful neighbour while he somehow managed, in spite of her protestations and gentle arm-slaps to finish a story about Leonardo DiCaprio hitting on her in a club in New York. The punch-line being that she didn't even know who he was. Marieke rolled her eyes as if to infer that Silvestro was such a charming liar but behind this mock-mortification her eyes twinkled.

My role for the evening I decided was to be impressed. Oh how wonderful it all was. How fortunate to be at the winning table with the Titanium, Gold and Silver Lions sat like ornaments on the linen. Oh thank you all for allowing me a seat at your table. And a desk in your agency. I kept one hand on the water glass making sure it didn't get filled with wine. People were very generous with booze when they weren't paying for it. Marieke suddenly became even more serious.

"Do you mind people drinking around you?"

"No, it doesn't bother me."

"Silvestro says you don't you drink at all?"

"No."

"Nothing?"

"No."

"Ever?"

"No."

"Not even at Christmas?"

"No."

"No joints either?

"No."

"You don't do *anything*?"

I'd already said it too many times but there was no other word for it.

"No."

This was not the answer she wanted and now having wrinkled her pretty brow I felt like I'd ruined the mood and I was ready to change the subject. Johnathan was looking interested in my direction. Christoph had put away his phone and Silvestro was sitting back in his chair the better to regard my discomfort. I was after all the only one at the table who wasn't on the brink of getting absolutely fucking sloshed. It seemed only fair that I should explain myself. I tried to think of a way to change the subject. The awards. The weather. The French. Her bracelet. Did she get it locally? Your bracelet, I like your bracelet.

"But don't you ever feel the need..." she paused here selecting and discarding phrases, "...to escape yourself?"

It was a revealing question. It told me that she considered it normal to want to escape. It was as if I'd caught a glimpse of her naked without her knowing. The thing now was not to be critical of her. A silence had descended. An answer was expected.

"Well," I said, now addressing the entire table, "I suppose I try to make myself more inhabitable."

Was *inhabitable* even a word?

Fuck it, she was Dutch.

I hadn't noticed until that moment that she

was smoking a joint so well-rolled it looked like a cigarette and the glass of white wine on the linen in front of her was so full it might have been water. Inhaling from the joint she raised her glass, sipped, swallowed, and regarded me anew. I didn't see her exhale.

"I like your bracelet." I said quickly.

This somehow signalled the all-clear and the conversation resumed around the table. I tried not to look too relieved. Silvestro was still looking at me.

"I hear you've written a book."

It was true that during a quiet moment before we sat down to dinner I had mentioned to Christoph that I'd written something but only because he'd asked me and I hadn't said it was a book. I said I'd written something and that I wasn't even sure what it was. Christoph appeared unsurprised but then as a producer that was his job. The file containing my book was accessible on the agency's shared network so it was possible Christoph had already seen it there before I told him about it. For all I knew he might have even read it. Either way he'd obviously mentioned it to Silvestro who, despite Lucien's best efforts to deplete it, still had money left in the Projects slush-fund. As he continued talking I didn't hear, so much as see, Silvestro's mouth open and close in apparent slo-mo around words that seemed to suggest that he might like to publish this so-called book of mine.

He would need to read it first of course and I would need to keep an eye on the agency in the meantime but maybe I could send him the file so he could get an idea of what it was about? He couldn't risk the possibility that I might put even less energy into the agency than I had already done recently and publishing my book would keep me motivated and give me a reason not leave them all in the shit. I was after all, at that point the only one beside Pamela who knew where all the adapts for the print work could be found.

I nearly cried when I heard him say the word *publish* because even though it was like a dream coming true it was cheapened by the fact that in doing so I might strengthen my connections to the advertising business when my intention had been to write a book that did the opposite.

"Can I think about it?"

"Yes of course, take your time. No rush."

He, of all people, understood the need to pretend to think about it.

Open on a wide-shot of me checking into a tiny little cheap hotel in a back street in Cannes. A shrunken old man in the tiny reception area hands me a key. Cut to inside the room as I enter and look around. It'll do. Shrugging my bags to the floor I make my way straight to the bathroom and after a few moments we hear two distinct unmistakable plops. There is a gurgling sound but the cistern seems to be faulty. I try flushing again. Nothing. I pick up the phone and when the old man at the front desk answers I confidently declare in my best French; "Monsieur, la toilette ne march pas."

Silence.

The old man doesn't understand. "Toilette. Not. Work" I say again. Cut to the wizened old man in reception as he repeats the phrase. "Toleet. Non. Quoi? Cut back to me holding a burning match to dispel the odour. I try once more to flush the toilet but with no success. There is a quiet knock on the door and I open it to find a beautiful young girl standing there in an apron. She might be the old man's daughter or grand-daughter or niece. She is smiling professionally.

"Il y a un probleme, monsieur?"

"Ah yes, over here." she follows me to the bathroom and when I nod at the toilet she looks away horrified. I wave frantically to regain her attention. I behave now like we're starting all over again and I raise my index finger in front of her face. I hold it there hypnotically before theatrically moving my hand towards the flush-handle and slowly, as if demonstrating to a child, I push it downwards. The toilet flushes perfectly. I stare at the toilet bowl in disbelief. The girl starts to cry. My mouth opens and closes as I try to find some way to explain. Learnanewlanguagedotcom

----

LUISA

The fact that MANG094's picture was fuzzy would normally have served as a warning but I had nothing better to do that Sunday evening after returning from Cannes and meeting her for a coffee would kill an hour or two before dinner. On the way there I found myself walking behind a small girl with an outrageous little ass. I remember being concerned about turning up late if I didn't overtake her but I couldn't bear to leave that ass behind. I looked ahead to the Anne Frank Huis where we had arranged to meet but apart from the ever-present carefully-curated queue of tourists I saw no one. The little girl in front of me stopped abruptly and took out her cell phone. I could see now that her face was pitted and pocked and not at all attractive and certainly not as young as I had first assumed. My phone rang and when she heard it she looked up and smiled.

"Hi, I'm Luisa."

She was from Brazil. They value an ass down there. I guessed she was in her early forties but she might have been older. She never told me her age and she seemed to delight in the idea that I couldn't guess. She did something indecipherable for an IT company in Amsterdam and as she explained exactly what this entailed I pretended to understand completely. She referred to her daily gym-visits as ass-maintenance. She was out of the country more than she was in it and when she returned she always had a new set of lingerie to model for me. She took almost as much pleasure in the beauty of her body as I did. She was addicted to the effect she had on me. I was a full-length mirror with an erection.

Her pockmarks blurred together when we kissed and refocused hideously when I pulled back. This drew me closer to her like an exhausted boxer hugging an opponent. She was so compact and toy-like I could fuck her and fold her away afterwards. She made frequent references to a breed of monkey called the Bobo who apparently gave each other blowjobs. I couldn't tell if it was a remnant from a prior relationship or whether it was just a cute affectation but she would actually use the term Bobo to describe a blowjob. Knelt there in front of me her with her face so firmly attached to my midriff she looked like she had a beard of balls.

Afterwards we'd sit naked looking out on the canals from the window of her apartment. We could see right up the Reguliersgracht. A pretty sight on a clear night. We ate strawberries and Ben and Jerry's and museli. It was the perfect relationship for me. Her body was amazing and her face was a built-in get-out clause.

"My doctor thinks it's a mess."

She looked directly at me, making sure I understood. What was a mess? Her face? Her health? What kind of a doctor would describe a patient's health in this way? The Dutch weren't exactly renowned for their charm but this sounded a little too harsh.

"So it's a mess." I said and smiled as if this was the cutest thing in the world. It was a weird moment because by now she was sitting astride me grinning and grinding herself down on me and I was seconds away from a re-ignited hardon. She seemed relieved somehow. Younger-looking. I smiled up at her and then hid in her hair as she began shoving herself back and forth on me. On my way home, as the effects of two successive orgasms wore off I realised I'd misheard her. *"He thinks it's M.S."*

Multiple Sclerosis.

Luisa was worried I'd stop seeing her.

She was right.

*****

The next day it was announced in a group email

that Silvestro was leaving. He had accepted a job as editor of Passione magazine in Rome. The email made it sound like he would be immediately replaced but it was just a smokescreen to keep the Olaffson clients from panicking. In fact, the New York office was already dealing with the logistics of closing the place down. And though there was no love lost between Silvestro and the New York office he didn't want to be sued for leaving them in the lurch so publishing my book would at least ensure my continued presence until the agency closed.

The files were already with the printers when he announced he was leaving. It occurred to me that in his new capacity as editor-in-chief of an internationally renowned magazine, a quote from him would lend some much-needed authenticity to my soon-to-be published book. I settled on a typographic style that mimicked what a real publisher might do and even I could see it was beginning to approach the coast of something that might not get laughed at in a bookshop. It was Pamela's suggestion to apply for a barcode and again I had only agreed because I thought it would make the book more convincing.

I opened the manila envelope that Johnathan had handed me the week before. Amongst the glossy enticements to work with the cream of New York's photographers, directors and stylists was a plain looking envelope with a governmental eagle embossed in the right hand corner.

My green card was approved.

Open on a shot of me reading a book. I'm looking rather smug. Panning around the apartment we see unopened cardboard boxes stacked haphazardly. They look like they've just been delivered and in one opened box we see copies of the same book I'm reading so intently. Diary Of An Oxygen Thief by Anonymous. Suddenly I'm distracted by muffled snippets of a flagrant argument coming from upstairs. Cut to the arguing couple upstairs. The fact that they are speaking Dutch adds to the aggression of the situation. English subtitles appear on the screen below them.

"What time do you call this?" the girl says. "It's our anniversary."

"I didn't forget I just bumped into Bob." says the man defensively.

"Bob? Nobody's called Bob any more."

"Bob…you know Bob, he asked after you."

"I don't care if Robert DeNiro asked after me."

She smashes a vase.

Cut back to me downstairs as I take out my cell phone.

"Yes I think maybe you can help." I say.

Cut back upstairs. The girl is shouting now.

"What I'd like to know is where you've been for the last four hours?"

"Three, actually.'

"Four, you went out to get a pint of milk."

"I got the milk." he holds up pint of milk.

"But I've been cooking all day, it's our anniversary…." Just then we hear the sound of a doorbell.

"That might be Bob for you now." she says sarcastically. On opening the door she is met by a huge bunch of flowers handed to her by a courier.

Assuming her boyfriend ordered them for their anniversary she throws herself into his arms. Tears of rage become tears of joy as the boyfriend accepts her sensuous kiss of gratitude.

Cut back to me downstairs. My smug expression has returned and I settle back into the armchair. I am about to resume reading when I hear the loud annoying creak of bedsprings as my upstairs neighbors make love. My plan worked too well.

Amsterdam flower delivery, tulipxpressdotcom.

And so, it turned out that on that last Friday in February, I alone, was summoned to the couches downstairs where Ted Lichtenheld waited for me; half-stood, half-sat, inhaling only when absolutely necessary the surrounding atmosphere of what was already in his mind, a quarantined building.

He presented me with a beautifully printed, crisp memo announcing the closure of the company that same day. I marvelled at the quality of the paper and the opacity of the ink. This hadn't come from our printer. An hour later my entry-card to the building was cancelled. Orchestrating a remote electronic lock-out from five thousand miles away was easy while meanwhile the printer upstairs hadn't worked since I'd been there. It no longer mattered. It was all over. The satellite had embarrassed the mothership by doing too well. It wasn't meant to win awards. Our little office was only intended as an outpost. We had exceeded our brief. The Cannes Lions had already been captured and tamed and were on show in the reception area of the New York office. We were told they'd been held up at French customs.

Johnathan, having been offered a position in the newly opened London office jumped at the chance to return home. But within two weeks of selling his canal house in Amsterdam and moving his family back, he was let go. They needed to get him out of his employee-friendly Dutch contract. But it wasn't all bad news. I received a hundred thousand Euros in severance pay.

JANE
"Has Sean Killallon taken out a contract on you yet?"

Jane Duncan, Editor-in-Chief of London's foremost media magazine AdVent, had just finished reading my newly minted book. A positive mention in her editorial section would be even more impressive than Silvestro's quote. But how did she know it was about Killallon? She knew better than anyone what went on in the ad game but even so, why was she so confident?

"Is it that obvious?"

"Frankly, yes, see page one-oh-nine."
I ripped open a box, grabbed a copy and opened it at that page.

"…had done Killallon a lot of favors."

It was nightmarish. It was the one word that shouldn't appear anywhere in the book and yet there it was. I tried to let it settle into me; the horror of it. Fighting the feelings would only make them stronger. I had to accept it quickly and then deal with it. How could I have been such an amateur? It was bad enough having typos all the way through but this was unforgiveable. A law-suit would generate publicity but not enough make up for the worry and stress. I had an overwhelming urge to run. Just run.

But where?

I was beginning to see what people meant when they said the book was courageous. I didn't like hearing this because *courageous* meant *risky*. I suddenly felt like a boring client who didn't have the balls to run a cool ad campaign.

Letting that word through was suicide. I kept returning to the moment I found out like a slow-mo replay of an own goal. Somehow it got through and it was now in all ten thousand copies. A glum inevitability descended on me like ash. I accepted my fate and assumed it into my character. It seemed logical to let the feeling of abject defeat settle inside me since it would obviously be around for some time. What would prison be like? Would I be expected to suck cocks? I had better get used to the idea. I looked at bananas anew. Would I be expected to swallow?

Yes I would.

I consulted porn for pointers. If my survival rested on sucking cocks I would take pride in it. It couldn't really be that bad. I mean at least I'd still be alive. Sort of. And I could always write about it. If my cellmate let me. I heard about a prisoner who had avoided being raped because he was funny. In prison, humour is as valuable as cigarettes. And everybody knew that a repeatedly raped prisoner didn't tell jokes. Talk about motivation to come up with new material. Maybe it was a clever attempt by Pamela to undermine me? Could she have been so devilishly clever? It was just a matter of removing the space between the words so that Killallon was rendered invisible to my endless wordsearches. I had checked and double checked so many times it was surreal to see it there in the finished book. But why would they sue me? For not liking them?

Meanwhile the tasty little blonde girl from the Athenaeum Boekhandel, one of Amsterdam's most popular independent bookshops, called and left a voice message. *"It's selling well, we'll take another batch if you have them."*

Oh fuck.

Open on a dizzying over-the-shoulder shot of me standing out on the ledge of a high-rise office building. I look distraught and dishevelled. The voiceover sounds like my own thoughts.

"This is where I'm supposed to remind you of all the wonderful things you have to live for, but since it's little late for that, here's a question for you instead. Are you up high enough? If you jump from this height you might actually survive, and we don't want that now do we? Yes, you could always come back and take the disabled elevator to the roof and roll yourself off but wouldn't it be better to get it right the first time? I think you need a few more floors between the pavement and the possibility of people saying *the fucking idiot couldn't even kill himself properly*. Come on, the stairs are through here"

This actually makes sense to me and as I begin to edge back towards the open window I realise the voice I heard wasn't inner monologue, it was a real person speaking to me from just inside the window.

And as he helps me inside I can see that he is a calmer more handsome, healthier version of myself.

He wears exactly the same clothes as I do but on him they look tailor-made. He is my better self. As I stand there still staring at him I am suddenly surrounded by carers and paramedics and wrapped in a blanket before being helped into an elevator.

Later, from inside an ambulance, I see my twin once again this time as he gets in on the passenger side of a champagne-coloured Olaffson parked near-by. Beside him in the driver's seat is a beautiful dark-haired blue-eyed girl.

They kiss hello.

A wide generous smile spreads across her face when she notices the resemblance between myself and my twin and I can't help feeling we've met somewhere before, or that we will meet soon. This notion has a calming effect until something occurs to me. I look upwards. The camera follows my eyes and we realise the car is parked directly beneath the window ledge where I threatened to jump.

They drive away smiling happily.

Olaffson. Protecting Your Future.

BRIDGIT (Part Two)

An apartment in the East Village for nine-hundred a month? It was too good to be true. There had to be a catch. Surely she was setting me up for some terrible revenge. Had I hurt her more than I realised? Poor thing. I had broken her heart and this was her long-awaited opportunity to avenge herself. She'd stand by as I gave up my place in Amsterdam.

She'd even help with my transatlantic move until at last on the same day I arrived in New York with as many boxes of my newly published book as the luggage-limit allowed, I'd be told there was no apartment. I'd stand there ridiculous, caught between countries, apartments and cartons of my self-published semi-fictionalised memoir. It would serve me right for not marrying her. When I finally met her to pick up the keys she had a baby with her in a huge carriage. I was not expecting this.

"I didn't mention I was married?"

So much for my image of her pining for me in curtained rooms. I peered into the carriage and from under all manner of expensive-looking blankets and toys emerged a tiny fist like a parody of rebellion and attached to it was what I could only describe as a bald blue-eyed miniature version of myself.

Why was she watching my reaction so carefully? Was this in fact my baby? Had she gotten pregnant and never told me? I tried to do the math as I smiled and wiggled my fingers in front of …

"What's his name?" I was looking for clues.

"Tarquin." she said enjoying my embarrassment.

"Tarquin. And how old is he now?"

It had been two years since we broke up. Nine months to incubate and.. .oh jesus, had she arranged to get me an apartment in her building virtually opposite her own apartment so I could take up my responsibility in parenting our child?

"He's ten months."

Ten months? Ten months earlier I was banging Rebecca. It couldn't be mine then. But maybe she froze some of my sperm. Was that even possible? But she was married. Or so she said. The baby didn't look too happy about the situation. Like father like son?

"Oh my god he looks just like you, congratulations."

This from the waitress looking at me and Tarquin like we were biological tennis. I had been lured back to New York with the promise of a cheap East Village apartment and now she was about to ambush me with a paternity suit. She was a lawyer she knew all about these things. She knew I had enough money to warrant the effort because she had already all my bank account details. She was laughing at me.

"Oh my god no. I see what you mean, but no, he's just a friend."

The waitress retreated. I exhaled. The truth as always, was less flattering. As an unemployed writer I fulfilled the requirement that all tenants in her building be of low-income status and preferably connected to the arts. Of the six apartments in the building only two of the occupants met these requirements and one of them was so old he was expected to vacate not just the apartment but his mortal frame at any moment. My addition to the roster would help reclaim some credibility for the co-op and with my recently banked severance money there would be no worries about me keeping up with the rent. In fact, if anything, I was the one doing Bridgit a favour. And so, within weeks I was back in New York under my latest guise; a writer living in the East Village.

3

PRUDENCE

"Are you Brent?' it was a woman's voice. I looked up from my double-toasted bagel and shook my head.

"No, sorry."

"Oh, sorry." she said, smiling weakly as she sat down at an adjacent table glaring at me like I had just lied to her. Should I double check? Was I in fact Brent? If she had been gorgeous I might have been less certain. Her face was a conspiracy of cosmetics and I could see how her online profile might attract some emails but day-lit and sitting across from me she looked like an effigy of a young girl. The door to the café opened behind her and the shaved head of man about my height poked inside. His eyes ricocheted crazily but the rest of him remained outside. When he saw the woman he stopped and his eyes met mine for a split second. He could have been an older version of me. Retrieving his head he disappeared. At least he wasn't fat. My phone rang and because I didn't recognise the number I answered.

"Hello?

"Hello darling sweetie it's Prudence."

It was the literary editor of the celebrated Prowess magazine and her little squeaky voice was even sexier now that she was alone in her apartment. She had already described herself as "the editor of a well-known magazine" in her profile so I knew after a only little research who she was before she called. Her voice was laced with sex from the moment I answered and within minutes she was describing her body to me.

"I'm lying on my couch in just a t-shirt and socks." There was a pause while I downloaded this mental jpg. "I should warn you that I have very visible veins I'm not proud of."

"Oh I don't know, veins can be useful..." I said "...all roads lead to Rome and all that."

She giggled delightedly, "...and when in Rome."

"Now stop that, I just don't want you to be disappointed when you see the real thing."

When.

As she continued describing herself she might have been reading a letter I'd written to a Sexual Santa. "And I have a very nice bottom. I'm always getting compliments for my bottom. My breasts aren't large but they're well proportioned, or at least I think they are, and my nipples stick out a lot, I have to wear padded bras because they poke out through my clothing and I have pubic hair. I work for a magazine that doesn't believe in it but I have pubic hair. I've been with men who really like it bald but it grows back you see…"

As I got up to leave I had to hide my hardon from the waiting woman and her accusing eyes. I walked over the Brooklyn Bridge to meet Prudence at the Henry Street Ale House and she turned out to be a lot smaller and prettier than I'd expected. She still had no idea I had written a book and so for every moment I withheld this information I felt like a liar. She was literary and tasty. Nice ass too. Lovely kissable lips and she was keen. Amazingly keen. She was very touchy-feely from the moment we met. She couldn't keep her hands to herself.

"There's a book." I said.

She seemed to accept the information quickly and nodded like it was inevitable. It was as if I had just told her I was married with three children.

"Oh there's a book is there?"

I was about to explain that I had no idea who she worked for when we first emailed but I knew it would sound hollow. We walked down to the promenade and sat on a bench facing the famous Manhattan skyline. The setting couldn't have been more romantic but when I leaned over to kiss her she stopped me.

"Be careful darling, you might cut yourself."

I was sure she was referring to my attempt at getting published but seeing the confusion in my eyes she added "...on my earrings, they're very pointy."

"Fortifications against unwanted advances?"

I was trying to impress her. She smiled weakly and looked across the river as if trying to decide what to do with me. We had certainly touched a lot for a first date. Up to that point she had seemed in a hurry to have me fall in love with her. I think what had impressed her most about me was the fact that I worked in advertising. Now it was beiginning to look like I was just another penniless writer. Pushing her breasts out she mentioned something about her shoulders being tight and so I dutifully offered to massage her compact little back. She was tight and muscular but not unpleasantly so. Her mother was a functioning alcoholic she said without ceremony. Maybe this was what was bothering her. That I didn't drink.

"She only drinks wine..." and here she left a space for me to say; "Oh well that's ok then." but I just nodded behind her on the bench. As she continued talking I began to feel genuinely sorry for her. Her job sounded terrible. Here she was, pretty, intelligent, literary-minded and funny, working for a high-end porn magazine. She took on the faraway look again when she spoke of a novel she'd written that had almost been published by Python.

"They wanted revisions and more revisions until in the end, well...they didn't want anything."

"I'd like to read it." I lied.

Then she answered the accusation I hadn't the courage to make.

"I can expose writers to much larger audiences."

She reeled off an effortless list of surnames and

then fell conspicuously silent the better to reap my amazement.

"That's some list." I said, only because I knew it was expected of me. I hadn't heard of even one of them.

"And John Banville has contributed more than one piece, you have heard of him."

"Of course I've heard of him"

"Thank God for that."

She was only half-joking. How would she introduce someone so literally feral to her friends? She was so small and tightly wound I said I'd help her uncoil but she thought this was not the most attractive of images. I said she took my meaning to be more serpentine than spring-based. I wanted to refer to my penis in this way but I thought it was too soon and then there was always the question of over-claim. For a penis to uncoil it would need to be a lot longer than anything I could muster. Mine was more likely to *depant* than *uncoil*.

She giggled wickedly and as I continued to massage her crackling back. I tried to sustain an effortless demeanour in an attempt at disguising my nervousness born out of the belief that I was being interviewed for the position of Writer.

She said she had smoked some dope the previous night after her dad went back to his hotel and I suddenly saw her for what she was. Not so much coy as I had first thought but conservative. She was capable of breaking hearts because her apparent openess would clam shut and leave the suitor standing outside and alone. Being a writer herself she knew I'd do anything to move my precious book forward, like a mother with a newly-born. So she can't have been in any doubt as to whether I was interested in her.

"You don't smoke?"

"No."

"And you don't drink?

"No."

"You don't do drugs at all."

"No."

"You're like a monk."

"My middle name is Camillus, my dad actually wanted me to become a monk."

"But Monks are allowed to have sex right?"

"Of course, you read the papers, we get more sex than most."

Her tight little laugh rippled throughout her back.

"It's just as well you're impoverished darling, because with all that charm you'd be unstoppable." This no doubt referred to my admission that I no longer wanted to work in advertising.

"And all the more impressive when you realise my penury is self-imposed, I'm merely being of service to humanity."

She wanted to see my bare head before I got on my bike so I took off my woolen skullcap and she ran her open palm over its surface.

"It's a nice shape." she said.

Maybe her dad was blue-eyed and bald too?

"It's because I'm a Caesarian; no forceps; untimely ripp'd doncha know, like McDuff." I felt fortunate to be able to harness my head-shape to Shakespeare; "In fact, I was as reluctant to enter Ireland as he was."

"McDuff?

"No, Caesar."

This referred to Caesar's hesitation in conquering a country he dubbed Hibernia (Land of Eternal Winter). If she didn't get the reference she didn't show it.

"Send me your book" she said stepping back and regarding me like an art exhibit Something had happened. Something important. It had suddenly become about my book. A major decision had been made. She made me promise to 'write her' when I got home safely. It was like something a mother might say. We had already hugged a few times and it had felt nice and natural and now that we were parting she seemed to want something more. It hadn't occurred to me to kiss her so I hugged her again, this time for longer.

"I'm sorry. I'm being quite huggy and touchy-feely."

"It's ok I'm not stopping you, I'm ok with it."

Not exactly gushing but it would do.

"Never mind the book I'm just glad you like my head."

"I'll show it to our fiction editor." and then added with her weak smile, "If I like it."

This was my big chance. I was sure she'd like it. I felt like it was the most important meeting I'd ever had. An excerpt in Prowess and I was made. A week later she emailed me in her official capacity as Literary Editor.

"We have a policy at Prowess never to print any material that is demeaning to women."

I never heard from her again.

MARIAN
I logged onto datemedotcom

0 messages.

I was sick of this. Where would it end? All this rummaging around in girls looking for what? Even as I emptied myself into one I was already looking for another. A life dictated by the gargoyle in my midriff. It had made sense up to that point since I had been so nomadic, but now I had a rent controlled apartment in the east village. To a woman in New York this was the equivalent of beer goggles. I looked longingly at the face of a beautiful dark-haired blue-eyed girl smiling at me from a profile called sculptorgrl82. It was time to unleash the most devious tactic of all. Honesty.

sorry but I hate this fucking site...please save me from the indignity of having to sell myself in this Meatmarket...we'll tell our friends we met in a book-shop...you need to know that you're far too beautiful and smart to be on this thing...meet me in the real world and I'll read to you in my Irish accent in my rent-controlled apartment while I massage your feet...anything you say...

Hi, yes I hate this site too, but I like the idea of meeting in a bookshop.

Her name was Marian and after a hurried meeting in the design section of The Strand Bookshop and a half-drunk cup of coffee in a nearby café she indicated a desire to see the final-we-really-mean-it-this-time director's cut of Blade Runner. I'd get the tickets if she got the treats. Perrier and pistachios. I couldn't be sure if she was looking for a friend or whether there really was some romantic interest there but I liked her immediately.

It was unusually hot for October and as she approached me in the crimson foyer of The Zeitfield Theatre she removed her grey cardigan and stuffed it in her bag. She wore a pair of short scuffed black boots with long black textured socks that stopped abruptly above her knees and silhouetted her beautiful slender shapely legs as she walked. With the cardigan gone I tried not to gape at all that clean skin racing up and down and around her arms, neck and shoulders and the outline of her small upturned breasts were easily discernible under the black sleeveless t-shirt.

"I neglected to get us treats." she said.

She couldn't pop into a deli and get a bag of nuts and bottle of seltzer on the way? I had already queued for an hour to ensure we got decent seats and now I was being told I was to go treatless for three hours in a pair of jeans that were too tight for me. I must have made some sort of face because after disappearing for a while she returned with one bag of popcorn and one bottle of Perrier and handed them both to me. Now I had treats but she had nothing. I felt like a selfish complaining bastard. But this was the moment she first exposed me to a smile that seemed to gather every molecule of my being around it like scouts around a campfire. Even the people in the queue seemed to shuffle closer. Now I felt like a lucky, selfish, complaining bastard.

She seemed to like me but I couldn't be sure if it was romantic. It had to be. Otherwise wouldn't she have to say something? Wouldn't she? But being newly arrived from Iowa she might not know the rules of engagement. Would I be referred to as a friend in her next carefully worded email?

It became important to understand what I was dealing with. Was she just looking for a friend? If so, I would need to be careful because this girl would be far too easy to fall in love with. In the subway seat beside me as we hurtled downtown I was treated to retina-scorching glimpses of her clean-skinned thighs as she rearranged herself according to the shift and shove of the carriage. It was like a dance. Did she know I was enjoying this so much? I had an urge to lift her straight up out of her seat and position her on my lap. The train's vibration would do the rest. She didn't ask one question about me all night. Not one. I even checked my reflection in the subway window to make sure I was visible. This beautiful uninterested girl unnerved me.

And it wasn't just me.

Other guys on the subway looked at her too. Long lingering wistful looks. They wasted no time looking jealously at me. I watched to see if she checked herself out in the subway windows. Did she derive any satisfaction from her image? I wanted to dismiss her as conceited. But she seemed not to notice. It simply wasn't her fault she was beautiful. In fact, if anything, she was careful where she looked. Maybe because she was so accustomed to being looked at she had learned to limit her options. It certainly didn't appear to be something she enjoyed. Male lust and female jealousy.

I looked like an idiot that night because I hadn't worn my favourite jeans. I had washed them specially but they hadn't been dry in time. And why had it been so hot in October? I began sweating when we had to scramble around in the subway station looking for the six train in the airlessness and at one point I saw her incredulous look as those cool blue-grey eyes registered the dark sweat stains seeping through my shirt like bullet-wounds. She was beautiful, calm and aloof. I was sweating. And as if to confirm this I heard nothing more from her after saying goodbye that night. Was that it? It was so rude. It was as if she had decided not to bother with me. It seemed so wasteful so Punk Rock. Gothic even. Had it really been my choice of clothing? For seven days and seven nights I ignored all sorts of primal and spiritual urges to contact her. If she had told me to fuck off and die I would have welcomed the clarity with hysterical laughter but hearing nothing at all was torture.

Your method of letting me know you're not interested (ie totally ignoring me) is uncalled for. If after reading the excerpt from my book, you got frightened, I guess I have to accept that, but it's a novel after all ...would you be afraid to meet the writer of a murder mystery? If you're not interested, period, then of course that's fine too but don't you think one short email is in order? You seemed quite down to earth to me, and I'm amazed at myself to be writing this email but I couldn't have you think I was ok with just being ignored...good luck.

My screen shuddered as I clicked *send* and as it readjusted there was an email from her. At first I thought it was one of those I'm-out of-the-office-replies but no, it was her response to the email I'd sent the previous week thanking her for a nice evening at the movies.

chiselling away on my latest piece...
i think it's likely i will be standing here at this same spot for the next 3 days...i'll let you know when there's a break...

Her friendly email arrived just as my pissy, self-centred bile-filled epistle went out. Had I'd received it ten seconds earlier she would never have known.

Encouraged, I asked if she'd like to visit the Met Museum during the week and her reaction was so half-hearted I suggested we do it some other time. She sounded relieved. It was as if I had freed her from a disgusting obligation; *Thank you for being so understanding* she replied. It stung that she was grateful for the opportunity *not* to meet me.

But such rebuttals only made me want her more. My biggest fear was that she saw me as a friend. That I was entering the Eunuchery. That I would fall totally in love with her while she sat there innocent of all charges. But that smile tranquilised me. What did it matter if I was only her friend? It was nice being with her wasn't it? We had a nice time together didn't we? I was enjoying myself wasn't I? The logic would rear up against the anaesthetic only to succumb to a pleasant complacency. Why did I need to fuck her? What was wrong with me? The act of having sex with her would protect me from being emotionally bruised. It would act as my deposit, my safety net. My safety-pin.

And then, during an impromptu meeting in a coffee shop, initiated by a text from her saying she'd unexpectedly found a parking space near my apartment, she let her hair down for the first time. She was beautiful. I had to actively wrench my eyes away to prevent intoxication. I could only afford to take little sips. She blushed noticeably and tilted her head in a way that gave me the impression she felt something too. Either that or she could see I was smitten and sympathised. Yea bewareth, step ye not so gleefully into the abyss.

I'd had plenty of time to prepare my defences against the paralysing effects of that evil smile and the hypnotism conjured by those vicious blue/grey eyes, so soothing and exciting at the same time, but now flanked by curtains of dark shining hair something inside me quaked. I was transported to my earliest memories of female beauty. Those pale tolerant understanding Irish girls modelling itchy-looking cardigans in my mother's knitting catalogues. Marian had the kind of face I could look at for hours and I used every conversational trick I had to do exactly that. She seemed aware of this beauty but determined to hide it.

Or hide from it.

From time to time she'd twist her face into an ugly expression to save me from the full brunt of her seduction. As if embarrassed by her wealth she needed to play it down. And the more self-effacing she appeared the more perplexed I became. Was she only interested in me because there were two more apartments vacant in my building? Would she suffer untold indignities to get into one of them? Was she merely waiting to confirm that I had money stashed in Amsterdam? After three hours walking around downtown Manhattan there was still nothing I could confidently point at that indicated I should make a move on her. Meanwhile her body language mumbled all manner of half-heard obscenities.

She pushed out those lovely pert breasts and twirled a finger in her heavy dark hair. She held my gaze in hers and refreshed her lip-gloss not just once but twice and when we stopped for a coffee she drew my attention to her boots turning them sideways to point at the frayed soles caused by our long walks and in doing so crossed and re-crossed those clean lean legs showing me far more than was necessary. Was she just teasing me? Was this something she got off on? I could plainly see other guys out of her periphery vision looking at her unhindered by any need to be polite. I looked for opportunities to move things forward I was still wary of being cast as the friend of this beautiful scruffy girl. When she made even the slightest effort she was stunning. And yes that smile was celestial.

Celestial.

I felt sorry for her having to be seen with me. It was obvious she could do so much better. Maybe it was because she had recently broken up with a guy who she described as *very pretty* and *very tall* and *very rich*. Surely I was just a consoling gnome trotting along beside her, yelping happily every time she flashed a smile. I didn't feel worthy of playing the male lead and yet I wasn't about to cheat myself out of the chance of getting close to that body either. If any sexual crumbs fell of the table I'd be there. She was definitely worth the wait, if waiting was what I was doing.

At worst I'd learn how to behave around beauty and I could use my findings on future prospects. In the meantime, I could at least pretend I was with her. She liked to walk around downtown visiting historic sites and I was quite happy with this idea because walking was perfect for making a move. And it was inexpensive.

But there was something nice about just getting to know her as a friend. Most of her friends were guys she said. This was an ominous sign. It meant women couldn't stand being around her because she was naturally slim and beautiful and men would do anything to get into her pants including pretend to be her friend. The last thing she said before disappearing into the subway station that afternoon was "I have to start looking for an apartment in Manhattan."

It was as if she wanted me to be clearly briefed. She was sharing with a roommate who she didn't get on with. Did she only want me for my two-bed-roomed apartment? Was I just a real estate agent in her eyes? This had to stop.

We went walking again and she looked great in her tight jeans. She had that tight little ass in there. God help me. She was so feisty and sprite I thought I had better make a move soon or she wouldn't be available for much longer. Some guy would approach her on a subway or in a café or in the street and that'd be the end of me. We sat on a bench in Union Square and as we chatted and laughed at the squirrels she played with her hair and shoved out those breasts and even touched my knee not just once, but twice.

"I'd really like to kiss you.' I said.

The squirrels froze in mid-nibble as an excruciating silence descended. It was so prolonged it seemed intentionally cruel. I should apologise. Make a joke. I had ruined everything. She inspected her boots. Feet together. I risked a look and instead of the beautiful smile there was only a lipless line.

"I'm not ready." she said, more to herself, than anyone else. And suddenly she just appeared extraordinarily vain. I had been reluctant to bring up the kiss at all but I was torn between a fear that she might be insulted if I didn't and a gung-ho need to at least get the subject aired.

"Ok," I said, "but I just wanted you to know that I'd like to."

There was a second uncomfortable pause and though I sensed my application was being considered, I'd had enough for one night. I had a sudden need to do some rejecting of my own.

"Alright then, let's get you to a subway."

After a joyless hug at the subway station where nothing more than our jackets touched I walked home feeling bruised and used but glad I had tried. I hoped I'd never see her again. I'd concentrate on my book. Maybe I'd use the AA meetings for contacts. There were so many well-connected people attending meetings all over the city it seemed wasteful not to approach one of them. I would routinely sit beside Cute-E, Simon Reeves, Patt Nillon, Anthony Sherts, Ulrich Wapton, writers, actors, models and millionaires. People less principled than I turned up at meetings pretending to be alcoholics just so they could network.

Years before when I lived in London, I myself, had sponsored the now famous Terrance Cutler when he first came into the rooms. It was obvious that in asking me to sponsor him he was looking to get a part in a commercial. And I, hoping to trick him into getting sober encouraged him to believe I'd cast him in something as soon as he completed the

Twelves Steps. But Terry was too clever for me. He had already taken the precaution of asking two other well-placed AA members to sponsor him so that he could decide which of us might offer the best career opportunity. He stopped calling after only a few days and I assumed he'd gone back to drinking. A few months later on a director's show reel I was faced with one of the most macabre images I've ever seen. Terry holding up a pint to camera. He had landed a part in a Blackbeer commercial.

The concept featured identical twins, both played by Terry, philosophising about the nature of dark and light while perhaps inwardly deciding whether to trade his sobriety for an acting career. The historic moment where he quaffs thirstily from the darkness is preserved forever. There's an ad for AA in there somewhere.

Can you forgive me for being such a teenager the other night? Although her text acknowledged my disappointment it still didn't offer anything even resembling hope. She was in town in her champagne-coloured Olaffson and if I wanted to go for a drive *she'd be game*. This expression had vaguely sexual connotations for me but I knew it wasn't how she meant it. And though I would have loved to take her up on the offer she had to be punished for refusing my advances. I felt I had to protect myself from getting any more involved with her.

Her offer of a drive felt like a platonic consolation for a sexually rejected buddy. I replied simply with a link to my acclaimed advertising website in the hope that it would show her I wasn't just some penniless idiot who should count himself lucky to be with her and that, if anything, it was the other way around. I hadn't really gone into detail about my advertising work because I wanted her to think of me as a writer. My intention now was to show her how cool I was while at the same time deny her access. I didn't think I'd ever be able to be so proud of my advertising work especially in art circles but it was beginning to look like I could.

An hour later, which in my mind, was enough time to check out the website and understand just how award-winning and internationally fucking wonderful I was, she texted me again; *the girl just wasn't ready...try again you will have more success.*

Wearying though it was to be proven right I wasn't about to refuse.

After a faultless dinner at the medium-priced Tibetan restaurant where we split the bill, I invited her back to my fur-lined lair. She looked lovely. There was something almost Midwestern about her manner as if she had yet to be Manhattanised. Her hair looked like Princess Leila by Pippi Longstocking. I liked it more when she wore her hair down because it framed that beautiful smile and made her appear like she was from seventies France but the significance was not lost on me that this was indeed date-hair. It was now just a question of where and when we would kiss.

There was a certain sadness attached to this realisation. As a lowly writer I was unkissable but she was willing to spend two hours on her hair for an award-winning advertising man. This was a nagging doubt that persisted even as I nudged her gently against the railings of Tompkins Square Park and in the cool January air we kissed for the first time. She flicked her tongue gently across mine and for a moment I wanted to just jam her against the railings but it felt too disrespectful. Instead we strolled back to my place pretending to be interested in what we saw on the way. I fumbled my keys at both doors and since I'd made such a big deal out of having bought Barry's tea from Cork she stood dutifully still while I went through the motions of putting on the kettle.

When I turned around it was into a deep longing yearning kiss. I felt her reach behind me to turn off the stove. She pulled back and looked at me now with the hope-filled eyes of a lover. No more ambiguity. Why? Because I had money? Because the apartment was nicer than she'd expected? Why did it even matter?

If only she had kissed me in Union Square.

I stepped forward and she stepped back and we waltzed like that kissing to the bedroom. On the bed we shoved ourselves together and opening her jeans I ventured fingertip toward the prize. I refrained from slipping a finger inside her, partly out of respect and partly from fear of rejection. Instead, I very gently traced that beautifully trimmed seam for what seemed like an inordinate length of time. The silence became tangible as if our futures depended on the next infintesimal motion of my index finger.

Had she known she would let me proceed this far? Was I just catching up with what she had already decided? Either way, the moment of immersion was audibly welcomed.

I can't say for sure but I think she might have come right there on my fingers. I say this because as I continued to touch her very gently she shivered involuntarily and moaned deeply like she was on very strong drugs. I was pleased with this of course and congratulated myself on having thawed her out at last. After a moment she arranged herself on top of me and lay there kissing and breathing warmly on my neck and ear. Her jeans were opened even more now and her groin was positioned directly over the hot bulge in my jeans.

"Let me introduce you to somebody." I said, trying to be casual but I was already drunk with lust. Deftly, she opened the top two buttons of my jeans and exposed only the tip of my cock and began flicking her fingers across it so maddeningly I almost came right there. I had to stop her. I wasn't ready for such an upheaval and I was enjoying the gentle unrushed atmosphere that had led us to this point. But I didn't want her to think her skill was unappreciated.

"I just don't want to come yet."

I was amazed at her skill. Amazed, thrilled and worried. If she was this good and that beautiful then I was in danger of…well…yes…of falling in love. But there was one area where she was still untested. If her ass turned out to be a misshapen mess then I could let myself off the hook, breathe a sigh of relief that could be presented as sexual satisfaction and turn my thoughts to the next online contestant. I let my hand stray downwards.

"Oh fuck."

She laughed but I couldn't have been more serious. It was perfect. Having all my criteria met was unsettling. I was like a castaway inconvenienced by rescue.

*****

I had only just arrived in front of the Metropolitan Museum of Art when I saw Marian approach in scuffed boots, woolen tights, leather mini-skirt and an open coat. For a moment I didn't even recognise her because she looked like one of those girls I was accustomed to seeing on the way to a date with some lucky bastard other than me. That she looked that good was in itself something to celebrate but the realisation that she had dressed like this specifically for me elevated my senses to such a degree that I gushed with gratitude.

We sauntered between the Greek and Roman statues that merely confirmed for me how well-proportioned and beautifully-made she was. Surely the music to which we moved was temporarily on mute. I pointed my camera at the statues but the pictures I took were of her. Smiling. Standing. Pointing. Walking.

"It's because you're so well-made, that's why you have such a feel for three-dimensional objects. You instinctively know when something is beautiful because it meets the standards of craftsmanship that you yourself represent."

Yes, I actually said that to her.

She beamed at this and stepped effortlessly into a rockstar pose with one hand on her hip and her head-tilted in mock-defiance. I took the picture that so many men would later drool over and I realised at that moment I was in love with her. It had been creeping upon me like the flu but now it was full blown. Almost as suddenly things started to disintegrate. We couldn't find a place to eat. All the cafes and restaurants were overrun with little nasal gnomes from the Upper East Side and the lovely Marian was starting to show signs of being seriously dissatisfied. Pissed even. Couldn't she at least pretend to be polite? Was this her real character showing through? Had everything else just been an act? At last we ducked into Casimir, which was far too pricey for my newly bohemian tastes but worth it in the end because after a burger, the cheapest thing on the menu, she was fine again.

"What would you like to do now?' I said, fully prepared to walk her to the subway.

"Lets have some more of that tea we never end up drinking."

There was only one response that.

Lying there afterwards I felt as if a huge magnet had been lowered over me and all the sharp metal filings and ground-down iron fragments that had been circulating in my body and mind had been magically lifted out and replaced with warm honey. "You're like a teenager." she said, blushing at the sight of my cock hardening again. Wearing nothing now but her dark gray woolen thigh-high tights she looked exactly like an ad for underwear I'd once seen on the Paris Metro.

"Hold that thought." I said, taking the camera from the bag on the floor by the bed. She arched her back and turned slightly sideways and this was when I took the second soon-to-be-celebrated picture. I stared into the camera transfixed.

I'd lost all interest in other girls. I hadn't even checked my messages for days. An uncomfortable notion presented itself. If I had a girl like this then I didn't need to be online any more. I could remove my profile form datemedotcom. I had always imagined I'd end up with a French girl, preferably in France with children that spoke French and yet it was ironic that Marian should look more French in this picture than Yvette ever did.

Surely I wasn't about to settle for an American?

But I wasn't in the bag yet.

There was still The Phone Thing. This was our shorthand for my inability to chat on the phone without becoming enraged. As soon as I heard Marian's voice I'd feel something like dirty water rise inside me like a tide; an inexplicable urge to throw the phone at the wall or out the window or just hang up.

When she gently enquired what the matter was I blamed it on the gappy cell-phone service saying it was just too frustrating not being able to hear her properly and that anyway I preferred it when we talked in person. This was only partially true. The real reason was unutterable. When she was physically present the combination of her scent, beauty and dress-sense, created a halo-effect that knocked her less attractive qualities into soft-focus. Those impossibly slender thighs extending from the ever-present knee socks countered any upsets caused by Americanisms like *hey you* or *goofball*. On the phone she had no such ambassadors. Her dismembered voice offered no protection from the fact that I was, for the first time in my life, not just in love, but in love with an American.

And it had become almost impossible to bring her to orgasm. She'd repositioned my fingers over an area that seemed so far north of where I would normally have set up camp I thought she was joking.

On more than one occasion she removed my hand altogether not so much in disgust as resignation. Didn't she realise she was discarding techniques that had worked for a large number of satisfied women? Apparently the "very pretty, very rich, very tall guy" she dated before me had actually gotten angry with her because she was taking so long to come. I feigned surprise.

"Angry? Really? Why?"

"Yeah, right? I mean, after all, it's my body."

Secretly I knew exactly what he meant. How insultingly boring it was to be down there lapping away on god-knows-what for god-knows how long, each moan from head-office just another false promise of promotion. But even as I made them I knew such protestations were merely last-ditch attempts at denial. I was in love.

Drama sought her out. Hardly a day seemed to go by without some new micro-castastrophe befalling her. The frequency of these mishaps would have been intolerable if she hadn't insisted on being spanked for her part causing in them. Each new incident quickly became synonymous in my mind with the image of her beautiful pale quivering buttocks. Parking ticket, (Spank!) cracked phone, (Spank!) lost wallet, (Spank! Spank! Spank!) I thought about hiding her keys just to encourage matters along but as it turned out I didn't have to. She locked us out of her apartment one freezing night and as we waited for her upstairs neighbors, I decided to cut my name out of a piece of card and spank it onto her ass until it was legible enough to photograph. I really was in love. Maybe next time I'd cut out a heart-shape.

And then the hints began to be dropped. If only her roommate wasn't always so depressed. How draining it was for her to have to continuously talk her off the ledge. Yes the rent was cheap and yes they were old friends but she was starting to feel like an unpaid live-in therapist. This was my chance talk about us moving in together. And when she began smiling at babies and old couples I could have at least feigned interest in starting some sort of family or supplied her with some sort of assurance about our future but I didn't. Looking back I can see that my continued presence online was a misdirected attempt at forming some sort of fall-back relationship in case Marian left me. Insurance against injury. Or maybe I was just addicted to online dating. One night, after checking my messages on her computer I forgot to sign out.

LAURA
Laura ...there you are... unsocked and depanted and all alone on a saturday night...wouldn't it be interesting to imagine your hands were suddenly my hands? We might need to discuss this further over the phone...are evenings good for you?

It was particularly galling of course because I had never have invited Marian on a phone-date like that. But the tele-sexual inference was nothing compared to the spiritual infidelity. I have since asked myself a thousand times how I could have let it happen. Maybe at some level I wanted her read it. She was getting too close. Or maybe I yearned for the familiarity of unhappiness. Preferring self-destruction to uncertainty. It's obvious now in retrospect that we were finished the moment she read that email but it took a year to sink in. To all appearances we were still together and she'd laugh and smile and even agree to help me reach an orgasm from time to time but she wasn't necessarily in the room when she did it. She made a point of staying clothed and if I tried to unbutton any item of clothing her free hand would involuntarily push mine away. A handjob is a great way to keep a guy at arm's length.

I tried to explain that I hadn't been looking for girls so much as customers for my book. She thought about this for a moment. She was trying to be fair. Why not give me the benefit of the doubt? Maybe I wasn't so bad, I had some good points. But how could I do such a thing? Didn't I realise how much I'd hurt her? She was forcing herself to try on my ill-fitting skin. To look at the world though my eyes.

"If that's true, then why don't you use me to sell your book?"

Was she was trying to smoke me out? Call my bluff? If I really was just selling books then I didn't need to be online at all and especially since the book was supposed to be written anonymously. I imagined what it would be like to click on Marian's pictures in a datemedotcom profile.

FRANCOISE
"Likes literature, cinema and sex. Maybe even all at the same time."

This was the headline for a new profile featuring some of the sexier pictures I'd taken of Marian. Her face was either cropped out or in shadow so that there was no chance of her being recognised and I was careful to ensure there were no reflections on any surfaces where her face might show. There were one or two pictures I'd taken of her standing in front of a glass doorway in the West Village where she was gently back-lit and in her boots and shorts she looked gorgeous. In fact, I flattered myself that the four shots I selected for this new fictitious profile were of a sufficiently high standard that the photographer who took them might at least be considered semi-professional.

Username
beautifullylit

Body Type
Thin/Petite (I get most of my clothes from the children's section of Old Navy)

Which Superpower I Would Most Like To Possess
To read minds.

Languages
French/English/Italian

Occupation
Photographer-Assistant-Model-Writer

Last Great Book I Read
Diary Of An Oxygen Thief by Anonymous, it's a little scary but brilliant too!! I highly recommend it.

Most Humbling Moment
I'll tell you later...it involves farm machinery.

Celebrity I resemble Most
After being told I looked like Jane Birkin so many times I looked her up, and yes we have the same measurements, so maybe there's something to it.

More About Me
Ok, the farm machinery thing. I realise it might be misleading so I want to make it clear. I wasn't disfigured in any way...my summer dress was sucked right off me by a potato grader...not as humbling in France as it would have been here (the workers hardly even noticed) but embarrassing all the same.

Favorite Onscreen Sex Scene
The best sex takes place on the cutting room floor

No messages. A twenty-three year-old purportedly French photographer-assistant-model-writer with a gorgeous ass didn't get even one reply? Was it was because her face was hidden? Maybe they thought she was disfigured. Even after adding the disclaimer about the farm machinery she was still getting no responses.

If, as I told Marian, I'd only been using datemedotcom to sell books I was now being asked to prove it. Reporting back to her with a result of zero messages and therefore zero sales seemed to confirm I'd been lying. *Hotlisting* was a way of showing interest without actually sending a message. It was also a great way to ensure Francoise's profile was visited by those eager to see who had hotlisted them. I selected every male I could find in the New York area. All were eligible.

From the hipsters with clever headlines (*this is your caption speaking*) to the old farts who didn't even fill out the questionnaire because they knew they wouldn't get a reply (*just looking*).

But still no messages. It didn't make sense. If I was hotlisted by a twenty-three-year-old French girl with the body of a supermodel, in varying degrees of undress, I'd feel duty-bound to reply just in case there was even an outside chance of fucking her. I studied the profiles more carefully and began tailoring emails to specific profiles; *If you liked Trainspotting, you'll love Diary of An Oxygen Thief.* I was about to send this message to an inoffensive-looking guy who most certainly didn't look like he was accustomed to being approached by beautiful girls when I noticed under the option to *Send him a message* there was a subheading *He sent you an email three days ago.* This was infuriating because when I clicked on *beautifullylit's* inbox it still showed *0 Messages.*

Maybe he had been disqualified for including his phone number and contact details. The site forbade people from exchanging such details because naturally enough this would put them out of business. But then below the inbox I noticed another option entitled *Preferences.* I clicked on it and there, slithering over each other like newly netted fish were hundreds of glistening emails. Seven hundred and sixty three to be exact.

I hadn't filled out the *Preferences* section because I had no preferences. The site was designed to allow only your ideal matches through and because I was looking for emails from anyone capable of buying a book I had no need of it. There were so many messages I couldn't quite grasp the significance of what was happening. My glee peaked and dissolved into fear. Would I be the perpetrator of my own undoing? It was flattering that all these men wanted my girlfriend but would this be how I lost her? I was struck by their good manners and etiquette. I was being given an insight into what it was like to be a beautiful girl in a world of salivating men. Hugely flattering but mostly frightening. I began to see Marian's position. Why she sometimes tried to make herself uglier. It was degrading to be sought after purely because of the physical shape of your face, body, hips and tits. But such ideas evaporated when I thought of the books I could sell. It was the digital equivalent of striking oil. I decided there was no need to tell her how many messages she had received. Not yet. I couldn't risk the possibility that she might put a stop to it. And it wasn't as if I was doing it behind her back. It had been her idea. In the end, I told her there were seventeen messages. This was flattering without being overwhelming.

Would she be curious to see if there was someone she liked? I know I would be. But then again the profile represented a twenty-three-year-old French photographer/writer not a thirty-six-year-old sculptor from Poland Springs. Mind you, I suspected most guys probably wouldn't give a shit once they actually laid eyes on her but it would definitely be a hurdle. And the more hurdles I could arrange around her the more fenced in she'd be and the safer I'd feel.

The book was already mentioned under the heading "Last Great Book I Read" but nobody was going to buy it just because it was mentioned. They needed more incentive. Maybe I needed to flirt with them. I tried to remember which emails had sustained my interest up to this point. I seemed to like the hot and cold ambiguity of the replies. The way they'd first agree to meet and then cancel *I'm soooo sorry* and take the sting out of it by adding the word *baby*. Could I pull this off? I strove to emulate this delicate paradoxical tone for my first customer whose headline announced a fondness for the work of Honore De Balzac. *I have a friend who refers to him as "Ballsack" if you like his writing you might like Diary Of An Oxygen Thief.*

Ballsack? Was I out of my fucking mind? A French girl would never say that. No girl would say that. I had been too obvious. When Stanley Kubrick created new characters he invented childhood memories for them; the school they attended, their first kiss, where they holidayed, their parents' relationship, a knee injury. I should have waited until the third email before blurting out the title of the book. *Hahahaha ballsack??? that's hilarious, I haven't heard of that book but it sounds interesting, I'll totally check it out.*

He was thrilled to receive any sort of reply from a beautiful twenty three-year-old French girl. It was becoming clear that another foolproof method for creating convincing life-like characters was ensure they had a world-class ass. After a few more attempts I settled on an approach that presented the book as a personality test, the reward for which would be access to Francoise, as I now began to call her.

Have you read Diary Of An Oxygen Thief? I find I can tell a lot about a guy from his reaction to it. Are you game? One guy asked me to elaborate on the farm machinery thing; *you were in france? is that your home? j'adore la france.* The fact that he ignored the salacious image I had inserted in his head just confirmed how dishonest these exchanges were. Any normal guy would be forgiven for at least referring to the idea of a semi-naked girl in a field full of French workers. The omission was so conspicuous it was like complimenting a stripper on her nail varnish. *I'll pick up a copy of oxygen thief on my way home.*

Laughter delicious.

The older guys were so thrilled they didn't care if it was real or not. *You're young enough to be my daughter but I'm ok with that.*

If a beautiful sexy girl recommended a book because it was a good barometer of character I'd assume she was just protecting her interests. Online dating was a treacherous conniving world where men would do anything to get into the pants of a girl like this. She was merely filtering the bad ones. It was a simple test to see if they were worth meeting. They would never suspect it was a guy posing as a fictional character suggesting they read a true story purporting to be a novel.

I was getting a glimpse of what it was like to be intelligent and female in a world of drooling men. Guys who had ticked financial or medical felt comfortable offering tips on how to improve my photography. Why did they assume they knew better than a student of photography? Because they were men and I was just some little bitch. One idiot suggested I boost the levels as if the shot was mistakenly shadowy. Then another guy pretended he'd read the book when it was obvious he'd only read an online review. I knew this because I had written it under an alias. When he offered to pose for me I asked him to send some pictures and he sent three pictures of himself naked with a huge frightening pole of flesh sticking out of his midriff. *So what do you need me for? You could fuck yourself with that* I demurred before blocking him. It was fun being female and beautiful. To actually be the object of desire. A living breathing potential possession.

One young guy volunteered to fly me to Mexico to see the Mayan villages while we got high on shrooms. Another guy older but well-kept, offered private boxes at the opera and dinner at Le Cirque, yet another, a businessman with not a suit in sight wanted to know my preference in hotels and my shoe-size so he could lay out some options for when I arrived. Young couples invited me for drinks no strings attached. Out-of-town husbands were careful to mention their expense-accounts. Filmmakers gave me two thumbs up. Architects wanted to know my plans. Journalists promised to report back. Chefs said I sizzled. Applicants all.

On the other end of the scale there were the less confident respondents. These were guys who knew they didn't have a chance but felt they better send something because hey you never know, she might have a thing for bald short fat older guys. I had the power to lift these unsunned and gnarly gnomes aloft. To absolve them. And grateful to find themselves within spurting distance of my mighty vagina they wobbled away to buy my book.

I wasn't sure how much of this was legal. I didn't want to get into any real trouble. Mischief was one thing but crime was another. It was as if I'd broken into some forbidden never-before-seen Pharoah's Tomb containing treasures untold. I felt an eerie sense of responsibility. Mustn't knock anything over. Just take what you need. I reasoned that if I just confined myself to selling books I couldn't be accused of desecration and would therefore be spared the wrath of the curse. It would be seen as artistic experimentation.

"Your Honor, I was researching a book."

But it couldn't last.

Marian would have to be told before it went too far. And when that happened I knew she'd want me to stop, which I really didn't want to do. What I wanted to do was select each state and systematically hotlist every guy I could find and recommend the book ceaselessly until I exhausted the cities, towns and backwaters of this wonderful country. After all, Barnes and Noble had stores in every major city in the US and I had access to datemedotcom's members in all of them. And if I could sell that many actual books there was no reason to believe it wouldn't do even better as an ebook. Of course I'd tell her. Just not right away.

I didn't overtly need to say Francoise was French in her profile, I merely included French in her languages spoken section, and being female, there was no need to send out initial messages since the men were expected to make the first move. Each email was subtle and polite on the surface but trace it back to its source and there was a stiffening dick. It was fascinating to watch these guys wrestlethe same subject I myself had spent so many hours trying to perfect. They approached gently as if nearing a retarded lamb and even though my headline was fairly bold, *Likes art culture and sex, maybe even all at the same time*, very few actually made any overt reference to it. There I was in my thigh-high stockings, virtually waving my ass in their faces but these mealy-mouthed modern males had been so consistently conditioned to conceal their true desires under courteous cloaks they made a girl feel dirty standing there in her underwear. In response to my beautiful jaw-dropping ass all they could say was I find you intriguing?

No mention of what they'd like to do to it or me? One guy, after going on and on for paragraphs about some excruciating pseudo-intellectual treatise on photography broke down and got to the point, *by the way, do you like to be tied up?* By the way? Surely this what he wanted to know in the first place. I responded, *no, do you like to be gagged?*

Delete. Block.

The guy behind the counter at St Mark's Bookshop was pleasantly suspicious.

"I know you're doing something, I just don't know what."

"It's crazy isn't it?" I said innocently.

"Well whatever it is, we're burning through the copies."

If she asked any of these eager customers where they'd heard about this little literary oddity they were not going to say a hot french girl with a gorgeous ass from an online dating site wanted me to read it as a prerequisite to fucking her. No. They were going to say a friend recommended it. This would translate to the booksellers as that most coveted of sales phenomenon - Word of Mouth.

It was becoming obvious that men would do or say anything to get into the pants of a twenty-three-year-old French girl, and it didn't stop at age fifty or even sixty.

There were no exceptions, only variations. One guy, a Brit, tried to play on my insecurity when he accused me of oozing entitlement He had guessed correctly that amongst the flurry of fawning emails such an approach would stand out. It was interesting that a Brit should be the one to take this approach; his first contact with the object of his desire was to attempt to instil in her a feeling of inferiority.

I had become that most dangerous of propositions; a beautiful girl with the mind of a man. Actress and Agent, Ho and Pimp. And as such I conformed effortlessly to men's stereotype of women; All women are basically sluts who barter their bodies to get what they want. No wonder I met with such universal approval. One guy sent email after email after email. What did he think? That I hadn't received the others? That he'd catch me at a weak moment and I'd let him fuck me? Far from being flattering, so many uninvited emails were frightening. It was as if he was trying out lines on himself. Finally I deigned him worthy of reply; *the book is about an older guy who becomes obsessed with a young photographer's assistant, you might pick up some tips.*

Ok he replied, *I'll get it today. I need some new fiction.* He didn't need to know he was already taking part in some.

Another guy wrote three weeks after he'd bought the book. *I'm still interested in getting to know you, what do I have to do?*

He was a sad-looking little guy. Bald of course.

Probably wanking off over pictures of my lovely girlfriend's ass. Of course he wanted to fuck her. So did I. He'd have to get in line. One guy was on the right track with *call me paranoid, but are you the author?* I thought he was onto me until he began to unspool a vertiginous scenario where he suggested Francoise was the French girlfriend mentioned at the end of the book and that she had written it anonymously pretending to be the oxygen thief.

I sidestepped; *so you think I wrote the book? I wish.* Two days later he sent a glowing review.

I think he enjoyed it all the more for having been introduced to it in such an unusual way. It certainly helped that the book talked about sex, dating and booze. Hardly a difficult sell on a dating site. In fact I was very often thanked for recommending it even when they knew they would never get inside my pants. A pretty girl hinting that a guy should buy something was seen as normal. The guy expects the girl to make him pay for something. To prove he's a good provider. Not only is he expected to pay he wants to. It's understood that the woman requires a token gift in return for her company. Tickets to the opera, or a concert, or a movie, cab-fares, dinner, flowers. All she is expected to do in return is look fabulous, nod a lot and smile as if she's enjoying herself.

These men were well-spoken, highly cultured professionals, occupying some of New York's top positions in the arts and media. They were what we referred to in advertising as opinion-formers. These guys were even more sought-after than the target audience because these were the people the target audience listened to when they wanted to know what was cool. You can feed a dog organic vegetables and over time he'll adapt, but put a steak in front of him and his true nature will show. These cosmopolitan journalists, architects, web-producers, lawyers, copywriters, designers, artists and entrepreneurs were salivating at the prospect of a superior piece of French ass. But even though the photos plainly showed a half-naked girl with a beautiful body they had learned through years of conditioning that they needed to feign indifference to her sexuality and compliment her photographic technique instead.

What would a photographer's assistant want to hear? She'd obviously want to hear how well her photos were composed. They were supremely confident they could dupe this inexperienced little fawn. At only twenty-three years of age she was obviously confused about how much flesh she should show, she was probably some rich French guy's daughter who had no idea how to behave.

Someone was going to fuck her so why not be that guy? Jerome Feerce, the award winning Creative Director of PDB and well-known author of sci-fi books, wanted to be that guy. A fifty-seven-year-old Swede, sniffing around the beautiful ass of my thirty-six-year-old American girlfriend, posing as a twenty-three-old French girl. I looked him up and yes he was married with three kids. Well so what? He was a bestseller wasn't he? He'd made it to the top hadn't he? This was Manhattan wasn't it? In reality, we were just two old ad-guys trading copy.

Meanwhile I'd look at Marian when she turned up to meet me and I'd have to pinch myself. It was as if I was going out with a model. A moody model.

She was even more beautiful now that I was losing her. I was that one guy amongst thousands lucky enough to be with her and she could hardly bear it when I touched her. She visibly flinched before I even made contact. I had caused this in her? She said it was a relief to talk to her doctor about a neck-ache because at least he didn't roll his eyes waiting for her to finish. This was a dig at me and I blushed in acknowledgement. But I had never really been able to follow her thread when she spoke because she jumped around from point to point without warning and when I asked for clarification she became irritated because in her mind she had already supplied this information and if I was asking such a question it meant I hadn't listened the first time round and if I hadn't been listening then it had to mean I didn't care about her and if I didn't care about her why was I trying to touch her? I decided to pretend harder.

But pretend to be what? I couldn't trust my perceptions any more. Did I only want to be with her because she was such a great sales tool or did I love her for who she was? Would she leave me in disgust as soon as she realised what I was doing? I couldn't even trust the enthusiastic responses to the book emanating as they did from libidinous men who would say anything to get into the pants of the girl who had made the recommendation.

The was only one irrefutable truth.

The sales.

And yea they were plentiful. I kept two pages open on my computer screen; one showing Francoise's profile with its constant supply of eager supplicants and another adjacent page showing the corresponding sales on Amazon. The main profile picture of Marian in her thigh-high stockings was like something by the French photographer Guy Bourdin and so I claimed it was a self-portrait paying homage to him. My book was now inseparably associated with two of France's most enduring style icons. Jame Birkin and Guy Bourdain. And all three were Googled accordingly.

In the meantime being with Marian was becoming impossible. There were too many subjects that couldn't be talked about. The silences grew longer and more impenetrable until they overlapped. We lied to each other by omission. The strange thing is that I got the impression we could have gone on like this for years. After all I didn't want anyone else. To me she was the perfect woman. Yes of course, I saw attractive women everywhere but compared to Marian they were just unknown accumulations of organs and limbs. They would never represent the bitter-sweet unknowable concoction that only she had about her; that exquisite confusion. Being touched by her had been a triumphant luxurious sensation. It was so flattering that she should even want to cause me to feel pleasure that somehow my guilt dissolved into gratitude under her touch. And there was that bottomless lust I felt for her, a spiritual longing that no mere physical exchange could extinguish.

But even as the sales soared and the reviews enthused I knew we had to make a clean break of it. No contact. It was the only way. We'd be friends, yes of course, but just not yet. It was too soon for that. For two days the relief was euphoric until suddenly an entire civilization seemed to burn down inside me.

Devastation.

In her cavernous absence I replayed and blinked away the awful moment she confronted me about the email. This would be my punishment. As the weeks turned into months we never got the chance to discuss anything because we were too busy I suppose, recovering from each other. In fact, this book is the closest I've come to letting her know what actually happened and why.

The previous year when things were still good we'd spent a lovely afternoon wandering around Williamsburg. It was one of those weekends where her roommate visited her parents and we'd had the entire apartment to ourselves. We had just had fabulous sex, or least I had, and Marian looked so effortlessly beautiful it seemed like we had stepped onto the hundred-acre set of a commercial for jeans or sneakers or maybe even a romantic comedy with an edge. The Williamsburg Bridge poked into every picture I took of her and we laughed knowingly at the very idea that even here so deep behind the Irony Curtain it was possible to be "in love".

I mentioned in passing that I played piano, that I had taught myself to play on a crappy old upright we had at home in Ireland an the fact that she thought I was joking seemed to indicate she hoped it was true. We found a music store but there was a sign saying no live music which still seems fucking stupid to me today but they probably had so many people jamming in there they had to ban it.

With great ceremony I invited her to step into a pair of headphones. Bowing her head she stepped forward into the coronation. I plugged the lead into a digital piano and I began to play. All I could hear were the keys fumbling and clicking as my fingers stumbled and drummed across them. I had no way of knowing if she was enjoying what she heard or if indeed she could hear anything at all but I kept playing anyway. Wary of missing a key, I darted a look at her.

The effect on her face was magical.

She had transformed into an amazed little girl. Her mouth had fallen slightly open and her eyes were wide in wonder. All the self-consciousness had peeled away leaving an innocence so pure it made me want to dance. I felt like I had at last found a way to communicate with her. As I sit her typing this I am reminded of that day.

I'd like to speak to whoever who put this profile together. It was from a forty-five year old entrepreneur who had posted pictures of himself relaxing on what looked like a yacht in what could have been the Mediterranean. He was onto me. Some guys might be very pissed off if they knew that their romantic attentions were in fact being pitched not at hot French twenty-three-year-old with an ass to match but a bald middle aged Mick in his underpants. Actually, I didn't even wear underpants most of the time.

As I see it there are four possibilities:

(1) You are the French girlfriend of the author mentioned at the end of the book and you are using your skills to help him sell the book. In this case using datemedotcom as a social media platform to generate an audience which is really impressive. You are beautiful and I'm sure it's working very well. You certainly got me. I would love to hear from you and meet you both.

(2) I'm wrong. You really are Francoise, a stunningly beautiful and sexy photographer who happens to be a fan of this book. I am not like the author, I've had different issues in my life which I would be happy to talk about. I would love to hear from you and I would very much like to meet you.

(3) You wrote the book. If that's the case you are a talent of unmitigated genius. You see, I too am the Creative Director and partner of an ad agency- production-company-internet hybrid, we have worked on similar if not the same accounts. The ad world is represented perfectly. My career parallels the timeframe in the book, I'm certain I would know your work and it's quite possible that we met. I thank you for exposing the book to me and for this exchange. It has been very engaging.

(4) You are the creation of the author entirely. Fucking Genius!! I am apoplectic. I can't tell you how impressed I am with the book but surrounding that content with this hook which brought me into it! Awesome. And the experience of engaging with you in this way via this character, spectacular. With the utmost respect, and if necessary - discretion, I would love to shake your hand and see if we might work together.

I hadn't thought about using this technique for anything other than selling my own book but it suddenly occurred to me that in the same way an ad agency could advertise any product as long as the approach was well conceived so could I with this more subtle method of covertising, sell anything to anyone. Would it work? You tell me.

*****

*francoise, just picked up the book this evening. looks
like an easy read. I'll get back to you with my thoughts
soon....so yeah, I guess i'm game....k*

*****

*listen, I would have written before but - uh - your profile
says you're looking for a woman....which sort of threw
me off because now you're all flirting with me.*

*****

*francoise...so, I'm also a big fan of films and sex. .and I
design books for a living, which makes me an automatic
fan (speaking of which... I just tried to order diary of an
oxygen thief and it says they're sold out !!. .and I hate
ordering things from Amazon). anywho, i'm intrigued,
how is your tuesday so far? best vince*

*****

*hello francoise.... well I've been spending quite a bit of
time on google this morning looking up guy bourdin and
that book you mentioned, as, no I haven't read it and
hadn't even heard of it. I see what you mean though.
looks pretty heavy and intense (alcoholism, abuse, photographers assistant etc). Unfortunately it appears to be
out of stock, so I may need to do a bit of digging around
to get a copy.*

*****

*uhmmm..I'm a little confused. You sort of asked me the
same thing last week. Did you get my response?*

*****

*francoise ...no, i dont know that book, looked it up
though and it sounds sizzling. is it still anonymous, or
did the author come out? have you been in nyc long?
where are you living? you can email me for real if you
like,*

*****

yeah, I'm game.... Just picked up the book this evening. Looks like an easy read. I'll get back to you with my thoughts soon. hope you're well..

*****

i will seek out the oxygen thief book at once, though it seems a difficult tome to locate. i do love a challenge. your guy bourdain tribute is striking ..are you a fan of baudelaire?

*****

hi francoise your profile is definitely intriguing but hard to see whether you have only one eye or not (then again one eye might be sexy ummm). Vous etes francaise? Je suis quebecois mais d'origine italienne allors je parle francais comme une vache espagnole. Let's talk oh mysterious stranger.

*****

Hey I'm studying to be a pilates instructor and was thinking if you needed to practice your photography it would be cool to take some shots of me doing my stretches.

*****

wow, devoured the book it in two big, greedy gulps, it's dark, smooth and jagged edged.like a fresh piece of broken glass that you want to touch even though you know you shouldn't.

*****

How come you didn't answer any of my emails if your going to hotlist me again? I don't mind playing around on here but its more fun if there is a dialogue.

*****

francoise, glad you still have all your limbs. Not that paraplegics can't be sexy too. taking any good portraits these days? intense book, do you really recommend that?

*****

*you're not very good at this, are you..? I see that you're
looking for a girl, not a guy..So, what's the attraction...?
just a playmate/friend? someone to borrow cool lenses
from? (you'd have to have a canon..) someone to make
your current girlfriend jealous.?what's the story...?
might I say that your pictures are amazing and I bet you
are too? what's your name? I'm allan ...when are you
free? today. lunch! 1pm...my place..?*

*****

*you got "woman" in your "Looking for" section but your
copy says you're looking for a guy. I'm above your age
range but you "looked" so I thought I'd wave and just
point out the gender issue. nice pictures.*

*****

*now that you posted pictures, I think I can fairly speak
for all lesbians when I say that they'd be more than
happy to have you playing on their team, if you ever
chose to I'll check out that book you mentioned.*

*****

*Eff...funny you should mention that book -- someone I
met at a party recently suggested I read it. I'm going to
look for it today and will let you know my reactions.
Then you can tell me what it says about me. It will be a
good exercise for both of us.*

*****

*hi there miss francoise, did you hotlist me by
accident? Jim (aged 60)*

*****

*hi beautifullylit, thanks for adding me to your hotlist.
and thanks for recommending the book ..it looks very
interesting you're smashingly cute, though I wish your
face were... um... beautifully lit rather than semi-
obscured. Is being a professional portrait photographer
as cool as it sounds? hope you're having a fun weekend,*

*****

the minimalist profile. it leaves more to ones imagination, a lost art really. you've clearly mastered the art of seduction through photos as well. i have no idea what you look like and my mind will wander endlessly until i do. nicely done, au bientot

*****

how's it going? I'm also a fan of art, culture and sex although not necessarily in that order and have kind of made a career out of two of the three. have you seen anything cool recently? your photos are very intriguing. do you have more? xoxo p

*****

yes I read it....enjoyed it...in about a day and a half. liked the nyc parts i recognized, and really felt for guy when he just wanted her to say "yeah, let's get lunch" but "no, sorry, busy, parents, blah..." ouch. among other excruciating parts. he certainly did get his, a lot of wincing on my part...good tour of the inside of his head...

*****

For more information about alcoholism and/or sex addiction go to aa.org and/or slaafws.org

V Publishing 20012 New York ©

For more information about Alcoholism and/or Sex Addiction go to; www.aa.org
and/or www.slaafws.org All characters are fictional. Any similarity with persons
living or dead is entirely coincidental.

CPSIA information can be obtained at www.ICGtesting.com
Printed in the USA
BVOW08s1146211016

465689BV00001B/12/P

9 780615 670195